truth

A **Confirmation Course** for **Teenagers**

QUOTE "Truth?" said Pilate. "What is that?" *(John 18:38)*
Jesus said: "I am the Way; I am Truth and Life." *(John 14:6)*

redemptorist
publications

Truth: A Confirmation Course for Teenagers

Published by **Redemptorist Publications**
Alphonsus House, Chawton, Hampshire, GU34 3HQ UK
Tel. +44 (0)1420 88222, Fax +44 (0)1420 88805
Email rp@rpbooks.co.uk   www.rpbooks.co.uk
A Registered Charity limited by guarantee.

Copyright © Danny Curtin, 2011.

First published September 2011.
Reprinted February 2012.

Layout and cover design by Chris Nutbeen.

Course concept devised, and written by Danny Curtin.
Additional material by Marguerite Hutchinson and Andrew Lyon.

Edited by Marguerite Hutchinson.

ISBN 978-085231-388-6

All rights reserved. No part of this publication may be reproduced, stored in a retrieval system, or transmitted in any form or by any means, electronic, mechanical, photocopying, recording or otherwise, without prior permission in writing from Redemptorist Publications.

The moral right of Danny Curtin to be identified as the author of this work has been asserted in accordance with the Copyright, Designs and Patents Act 1988.

The scripture quotations contained herein are from the New Jerusalem Bible, except for readings for liturgies which are from the Jerusalem Bible, with psalms taken from the Grail Psalms. Used with permission.

Redemptorist Publications is grateful to acknowledge the assistance of the following people in the development of *Truth*:
Fr David Parmiter, Canon Frank Harrington and the parish of St Dunstan's, Woking, as well as
John Toryusen, Rebecca Barber, Monica Conmee, SS Mary and Joseph, Poplar, Stephen Byrne and pupils of Gumley House School, David Beresford, Elizabeth Ridley and Michael Doherty.

The DVD which accompanies this programme was produced for Redemptorist Publications by Bob Walters at Digital Media Production and Training: www.bobwalters.co.uk

The publishers also wish to thank the following for their gracious assistance in making this possible:
Paula Macquieira and Carl Fisher at St Matthew Academy, Blackheath
Barry O'Sullivan at Nicholas Breakspear School, St Albans
Rachael Blackburn and Gerard Shepherd at St Mary's Catholic Comprehensive School, Newcastle

Katherine, John Jo, Conor, Vicky, Hugh, Mwende, Michael and Nicolette for taking part, and their parents for granting permission for their images to be used on the DVD and within the books.

The DVD was filmed on 5 and 6 July 2011 at SPEC, a vibrant Catholic community working with young people from parishes and schools from the ages of 7-18 years. Our thanks, sincerely, to Jon Rogers, Terry Toolan and the team there.
www.spec.org.uk

A CIP catalogue record for this book is available from the British Library

Printed by Advent Colour Ltd, Andover SP10 3LU

About the author

Danny Curtin has spent more than a decade working in Catholic youth work and parish evangelisation and catechesis. His experience working in parishes and the Diocese of Westminster led to him joining the Young Christian Workers (YCW). He became YCW National President (2005-2010) and worked with thousands of young people across the country and the world. This confirmation course is based upon materials he developed at this time.

During his time with YCW, Danny developed a great passion for working with hard-to-reach young people, especially those who are disadvantaged and overlooked in society. As a result, in 2011, Danny helped to found Million Minutes, a charity that seeks to support projects which transform young people's lives.

Danny was also the founding Vice-Chair of the Catholic Youth Ministry Federation (CYMFed) and co-author of 'Mapping the Terrain', the CYMFed research project into the life and faith of young Catholics in England and Wales in 2010.

Danny now works on a freelance basis with many Catholic organisations, charities and dioceses, helping them in their mission within the Church.

twitter
#truthconfirmation

QUOTE "The truth will set you free."
John 8:32

truth
A Confirmation Course for Teenagers

Contents

	Introduction	*page 6*
1	**Session 1 - Our Journey** *Our aspirations and what God wants in our lives.*	*page 13*
2	**Session 2 - Baptism** *We are valued and chosen by God and our baptism marks the beginning of our lifelong membership of the Christian community.*	*page 23*
3	**Session 3 - Confirmation** *Why do you want to be confirmed? Finding out what happens at your confirmation.*	*page 35*
4	**Session 4 - Getting it Right** *How to follow Christ in our everyday lives. How the sacraments help us to live our Christian commitment.*	*page 49*
5	**Session 5 - Preparing for Reconciliation** *Resources to prepare a service of reconciliation.*	*page 61*
6	**Session 6 - Time Out - Prayer and the Mass** *Thinking about our first Holy Communion. Examining how the Mass offers us the chance to take time out to think about our priorities and to pray.*	*page 69*

7 **Session 7 - Faith... in what?** *page 79*
Examining your beliefs and what shapes them.
Thinking about what is most important in life.
Looking at the promises made at Confirmation.

8 **Session 8 - Preparing the Confirmation Mass** *page 91*
Resources to help prepare the liturgy of the word at the Confirmation mass.

9 **Session 9 - Actively Living Life (post-confirmation session)** *page 99*
What makes a leader?
How can we be Christian leaders?

Appendix 1 *page 108*
Suggested texts for Reconciliation service

Appendix 2 *page 113*
Suggested texts of Confirmation Mass

Appendix 3 *page 122*
Resources to support a group after confirmation

Introduction

How to use this book

This book has been written to help you to run a successful confirmation programme in your parish. All the ideas in *Truth* have been used by many parishes before they were written into this book. So if you do want to do all the sessions, using all the materials in this book, you will find everything you need here to make your confirmation programme challenging and inspiring for your group of young people.

You are the expert on what will work in your parish. Once you have met your group you will also be the expert on what will work with your group of young people. All the information and ideas in this book are meant to help you, not to constrain you. If there are sections you don't feel will work with the people, or the resources, or the physical environment you have in your sessions, you don't need to use them. If you want to do a different number of sessions or arrange them in a different order that's fine too.

My journal

There is a journal for candidates which accompanies this course. It is designed to look fun and accessible. It contains more prayers, more information, and more inspiring quotations and Bible readings for each session. Each candidate in your group will need a copy. It is theirs to personalise, scribble on or jot down notes. It isn't a school book. It is their book to do with as they wish. They will need to use the book during the sessions in your group but they can also use it outside the group as a source of inspiration. We hope that by customising their copies and making their book their own, they will keep it as a reminder for years to come of the spiritual journey they have been on.

In this catechist's guide we have included a vertical yellow bar beside text which is also to be found in the candidates' journals.

See - Judge - Act

All too often, as Catholic Christians we struggle to find a way to balance our faith and the reality of our everyday life. We know about the truth of our faith. When we start living our lives from this perspective we know that we should always strive to live in ways which reflect our God-given dignity, and always try to promote the dignity and worth of others. However, the reality of our everyday life can sometimes take over. In our homes, places of work, study and leisure, we don't always see the dignity and worth that God gave us. Sometimes we strive to live our lives in ways that ensure our own personal security in monetary wealth, material possessions, or power.

If we ask any fourteen- or fifteen-year-old what the truth of their everyday reality is, we will hear back many, many positive aspects of life. But we will often also hear a list of heartbreaking facts: pressure from parents to succeed, expectations from peers to act in certain ways, bullying, violence, abuse of so many kinds, and escapism into today's world of ceaseless entertainment or of alcohol, sex and sometimes drugs. Often they will also tell us that they desire success, and with that often comes the desire to have security in money, a big house and the perfect relationship. Nothing wrong on the surface, and nothing for us to criticise, but we must ask: is this all that God wants for us?

Our task, when working with young confirmation candidates, is to enable these two starting points – faith and real life – to come together. We can bring the truth of our faith into every aspect of our everyday reality so that we are building our lives on one foundation stone, with our faith in Jesus Christ affecting every aspect of our daily reality.

This can't be done by just teaching our young people the truths of faith. Simply teaching teenagers about the faith will not enable our young people to experience that faith in their everyday reality. Neither can we solely focus on the experience of the young people and their opinions. Each of these approaches lacks what the other contains. The doctrinal, teaching approach concentrates on the truth of faith, and can fail to transfer any of that truth into the reality of the young people's lives. The experiential approach quickly turns into a discussion where everyone's opinion is valued, but no real proclamation of Christ is achieved.

The two can come together. We can ensure that the Word of God and the teaching of Christ are heard in the midst of young people's experience. Then they can enquire into it, and see the relevance of their faith in their lives. Following this, these young people can commit themselves to action and to living the faith, so that the truth of our faith can be lived in their everyday reality.

For example take the Holy Spirit. Simply teaching about the Holy Spirit could easily end up with the doctrine on the Holy Spirit becoming some external concept that has no part in or relevance to the young person's life. But if we start with experience, we need to ask: what occurs in young people's lives? When in their life do they need to make decisions, or need courage, or need to be strong? When do they gasp in awe and wonder? What knowledge do they cherish the most? These, just some gifts of the Spirit, can be identified in young people's lives, before moving on to our doctrine, and the fact that we have an advocate to help us in all these areas. Are we aware of this great gift? If not what can we do about it? How can we notice the work of the Spirit in our lives… how can we act in different ways… how can we ask him for help…?

This is the method of enquiry and action developed by the movement of Young Christian Workers (YCW), in which I was privileged to have the role of National President for five years. The YCW exists to enable young people to be trained to be apostles: young Christian leaders in life. The method is known as See-Judge-Act. In this simple approach we discover a practical catechesis perfect for confirmation preparation, wherein candidates commit themselves to living out the faith they receive. In this sense, we can begin to address the dilemma of confirmation, so often termed the "sacrament of exit". Rather, it can become the confirmation of the vocation received at baptism: to live as disciples of Christ. Instead of viewing confirmation as an adult faith-commitment ceremony (it cannot be this once we realise that some dioceses confirm candidates as young as seven), we embrace an understanding of the sacrament as an occasion when the candidate is empowered, through the specific gifts of the Spirit, to live out the Christian vocation they received at baptism. They are anointed and given the specific task of fulfilling their baptismal reality, and working to build up the Kingdom of God in the world.

One of the reasons that many dioceses choose to confirm at an older age is so that the candidates have a fuller understanding of what is happening. No sacrament is a magic moment with magical changes effected in the candidate. Most especially in confirmation the candidates need to co-operate in the work that God is doing through the sacrament, and allow the Holy Spirit to work within them. So, all confirmation candidates need to enquire into their own lives, and see how God works in their life, and what their response to God should be. See-Judge-Act is the ideal method to help young people do this:

- We **see** the importance of realising our own reality: Who am I? What do I want in life? What is my reality? What occurred at baptism? What will occur at confirmation?
- We **judge** what God wants for us in living that reality out: What does God want for me? How does God help? What is the role of faith and the sacraments in my life? What is my response to God's loving help?
- We **act** to link our life and faith: What can I do, through Confirmation, to be happy and help others to be happy? How can I help? How can my faith change things?

See Appendix 3 for more information on the YCW and supporting your group after Confirmation.

Role of the catechist

It is helpful, as a catechist, to imagine yourself with the specific role of being a "companion". A companion is one who travels along with someone – who shares the same bread (in Latin, *companis*: *cum* = with; *panis* = bread). Catechists who view themselves also as companions will balance their own experience, wisdom and commitment in their own adult faith with the patience, dedication and sensitivity needed when working with young people who are often searching, hesitant and questioning. It follows the example of Christ in the Gospels who showed great faith in the disciples he called (who were probably young), despite their questioning, misunderstanding and failures.

This helps with the See-Judge-Act methodology. For example, as adults we do not really know the reality of the young people we are working with. It is important that we accept this. Only the young people know their own reality, and so it is the young people who will learn from each other and grow together through their enquiry into life, reflection on faith, and commitment to lived Christian action. The adult's role, then, is to be a companion and:

Listen
- to take the attitude of a listener who is ready to understand their life;
- to always begin with acceptance of young people as they are.

Help
- to help the young people to speak;
- to ensure one or two young people do not dominate;
- to invite them to stop and think, to analyse and try to solve difficulties;
- to help them to express their experiences and their faith;
- to help the young people to see their projects through to the end.

Encourage responsibility
- to enable the young people to take an active role;
- to enable young people to "lead" their group discussions
    (this can work particularly well if someone is dominating – suggest they lead the conversation with the specific role of ensuring everyone speaks!)
- not to take over from the young people in their action and decisions, nor overrule them;

- to be concerned that the young people grow in responsibility;
- to pay attention to the fact that responsibility in faith cannot be separated from responsibility in everyday life.

Take part in the formation and education of the young people
- to play a significant role in their faith formation;
- to ask questions which help to deepen reflection and contrast life experience with the Christian values of the Gospel;
- to help the young people to be more sensitive to and aware of their situations.

Sustain
- to give lots of encouragement;
- to support the continual review of their weekly actions;
- to give moral guidance and support;
- to awaken and encourage initiatives;
- to accompany the young people in an experience of a missionary Church.

Preparing the sessions

Although this book gives you all the information you need to run the course, you will still have a little preparation to do. Each week, the materials you will need to run the session are listed at the beginning of each chapter. Try to look at this long enough in advance to get the materials ready in time, or you might have to make a last-minute dash to the shops!

Spend time reading through the material for each session well before the day of the session. Try to make the content your own as much as possible. This will help you create a relaxed environment where a conversation can take place among the young people. When it comes to preparing the Confirmation Mass, there is some important forward-planning advice on page 93, of which you may wish to be aware.

Before the course begins you may wish to meet with all the catechists to plan at least the first session and to think about other issues. Some things you might like to consider are:
- Do your group already know each other: are they from the same school, or even the same class? If they all know each other already you won't need much "getting to know each other" time and you might not want to do the activity suggested for each session as an icebreaker. Alternatively, you might want to consider mixing the group out of their usual friendship groups to ensure everyone engages. If they don't all know each other, or if there are just a few teenagers who come from a different school, it is really important to spend a lot of time on "getting to know you" and small-group work.
- What are the facilities like? Does this affect what activities you do? For example if space is extremely limited you might not be able to do some of the "To get us started" activities, or if it is a huge space you might need to think creatively about how to generate a prayerful atmosphere for the final prayer session.
- How big is the group? This course will work with any size of group, but you will frequently need to get the group into pairs or small groups so that they can discuss things well. If you have enough catechists you might like to assign a catechist to each small group for some of the activities and discussion topics.
- It often works best to keep the same groups each session, with the same supporting catechist. This helps to build relationships and to form trust among the group. At times

it may seem difficult to get conversations started. Don't worry and don't be afraid of silence. Gently encourage people to contribute by asking questions. Resist the temptation simply to talk, and to fill the silence by saying what you think. Don't be too concerned if one or two young people seem not to want to talk, and don't assume that they are not engaged. Some will be shy, others may find that someone else always makes their point first.
- What times and dates are the sessions going to take place? Does this affect the structure of the course? For example, if you only have hour-long sessions you will find you need to miss out some sections of each session; if you only have six sessions, you will need to prioritise which sessions to run and which to miss out.

Structure

Truth is made up of nine sessions. Eight of these are preparation for the sacrament of confirmation and the final session is a post-confirmation session, to allow the young people to reflect on their confirmation and what it means for the rest of their lives.

Each session contains different sections. While sessions are similar in structure to one another, they aren't all the same. Here is a brief outline of a typical session and how to use it:

Leader's reflection: this is for the leader's own personal reflection and is not intended to be shared with the group of young people. If you have a group of catechists, you could use this reflection as the starting point of a discussion between you when preparing the session.

Opening prayer: this is here if you like to begin with a prayer. There is a longer and more formal prayer section at the end of each session, so if you don't feel it helps your group to gather and begin with a prayer you do not need to use this opening prayer.

"To get us started…" activity: these fun group activities have been chosen to help the group get to know each other and have fun. There is often a serious point linking the game to the theme of the session.

See: this section always encourages the young people in your group to think about something that is going on in their lives, examining their behaviour and their beliefs. If you find very serious issues being raised in this session, you might want to spend extra time working on this.

Judge: this section encourages the group to use scripture and church teaching as a guide to their lives. The group can then link what their faith says to what is going on in their lives.

Act: this is the natural follow-on from the previous two sections: once they have thought about what is happening in their lives and what their faith says, they can choose how to act. Each session features a real-life story of someone who has used their faith to guide their life. The group are then encouraged to think of personal actions, and group actions.

Final prayer: each week a short prayer and scripture reading section is included. You might want to make this a big feature of the course, preparing an area of the room or the church to create a good atmosphere for prayer and reflection. You might want to think about lighting, music, images. You could use other prayers and have some quiet time for meditation too. There are more prayers and Bible readings in the candidates' journals which you might like to use if you want to expand this section.

The DVD

The DVD which comes with this programme can be used to encourage the small-group work. Show the DVD to the whole group (when you see the DVD symbol in this book) before splitting into smaller groups. The comments made by the young people featured on the DVD are unscripted, and were their honest reactions to the questions. As such they will help to inspire and challenge the ideas and reflections from the young people in your group.

Supporting the programme

Depending on the nature of your parish there are lots of activities you and your group could organise to support this programme. By getting the group involved in something more than weekly sessions for a couple of months, you might find they get more engaged with their sacramental preparation. Here are a few things you could do:

Service projects

Is there a project the group could take on? The best service projects are ones which help the young people to see the practical relevance of their faith. Choose projects that allow them to see the difference they are making and are not simply token gestures. For example, if your parish hasn't got a welcome ministry, can the group help to start one by welcoming people at the door of the church and handing out hymn books? Or it could be something that enables the whole parish to see the value, faith and commitment of the group. They might want to organise an event for the parish, a Mass, or get involved in a community project such as volunteering with elderly people, or providing assistance at the primary school.

On-Location sessions

Some parishes have their sessions on a Saturday or Sunday afternoon and visit a different location each time, which has some relevance to the theme of the session. So, for example, visiting a charity that works with people who have learning disabilities may link to reflecting on the gifts each person receives and how they put them into practice (e.g. in Session 3). The location needs to have suitable meeting space to complete the group-work for the session.

Social events

Is there an opportunity to organise social events as part of the confirmation programme in your parish? This could be something which is just for the group to enjoy together like a trip to the cinema or bowling or a pizza night. Or it could even be a social evening which the young people organise and to which their families are invited: perhaps a barbecue or a talent night, or a charity fundraising event.

Retreat

Some parishes have the resources to take their confirmation group on a weekend or a day retreat. The sessions in this book could be used in a retreat setting just as easily as in a weekly meeting in the parish.

SESSION 1

Our Journey

Session 1
Our Journey

Aim:
To help the young people recognise our identity as children of God, and how God wants us all to share in God's dream for our lives.

Leader's reflection:
What did you want to be when you were growing up? Have you realised your dreams? Or has life taken you on a different path from that which you would have chosen yourself? Whatever direction life takes us in, and whatever our circumstances, the Lord calls each one of us to follow him, and to get to know him personally. Following him means being able to discern his call for our lives. How can we do this? How can we become the people God wants us to be? This first session on our journey towards confirmation with young people explores these questions. It should help you to open a conversation with the young people about their hopes for the future, and get them thinking about how God might be at work in their lives.

> **TIP** "If there's a team of catechists in your parish, perhaps you could meet together for a few minutes before every session and read and think through the leader's reflection each week?"

You will need:
- A candle and something to light it with
- Some relaxing/meditative music
- Flip-chart paper and pens
- Small pieces of paper for the young people to write their prayer intentions on and some pens/pencils to write with
- A basket or something to place the prayer intentions in at the end of the session

Candidates will need:
- Their candidate journal and a pen

QUOTE "Love is from God and everyone who loves is a child of God and knows God."
From the First Letter of St John

Begin with a prayer…

As the young people begin to arrive have the lights in the room dimmed, a candle lit in the centre. As each person arrives, invite them to sit quietly in a circle around the candle. Perhaps play some reflective music in the background.

> Lord God,
> As we begin this journey of faith together, we ask you to guide us along the way, and be patient with us as we follow. Support us, Lord, as we begin to ask questions, as we discuss issues and as we grow in our faith. We pray that you inspire us, Lord, to be open to your leadership in our lives. Amen.

> **TIP** " This prayer is also printed in the candidates' books. Perhaps ask one of the young people to pray it out loud while everyone adopts a posture of their choice, conducive to prayer. "

Break the ice…

Introduce yourself to the group. Introduce any other catechists or helpers too. Welcome the young people. Tell them how glad you are to see them and how you are looking forward to travelling on their journey to the wonderful sacrament of confirmation with them.

This is a good time to mention any "housekeeping" items: from how many sessions there will be and what dates and times they will be on, to where the toilets are and whether there will be a break in the middle of today's session.

To get everyone started, begin with a group exercise to help everyone feel comfortable in each other's company and get to know one another a little. Use the following icebreaker, or another one of your choice. For this activity, if you have a large group you might want to split them into smaller circles of six to eight people.

- Standing in a circle, at precisely the same time everyone starts to say out loud how they define themselves. For example: "My name is John; I am fourteen years old; I live in Warwick Avenue; I have a pet dog; my favourite colour is blue; I am good at maths but not good at French."
- As they are speaking (not shouting!), encourage the group to make eye contact and really address each other, even though they can't necessarily hear what other people are saying. Also encourage them to really try to make themselves understood, even though the other person is trying just as hard to speak to them.
- This continues for a few minutes, until everyone stops at precisely the same time, shuts their eyes and stands absolutely still. (You'll need to agree how you'll indicate these few minutes are over.)
- Ask the group to notice their posture, breathing etc, and to notice how much they hang on to their identity. Notice, too, how "noisy" competing identities are. When they open their eyes invite them to sit for a moment of silent reflection.
- Now get them to take it in turns to introduce themselves to the rest of the circle.

SEE

In this section we encourage the young people to examine the things that happen to them in their lives and the lives of those around them.

What are the things in our lives that give us happiness? Friendship? Games consoles? Holidays? Allow a few minutes to give the young people some thinking time. Encourage the young people to make notes in their journals. Read aloud the following questions and discuss them in the group. We'll return to them in section 5 as a basis for thinking about what action we could take this week.

"What makes you happy?"

Ask the young people to think on their own and to write in their journal.

- Think of something you have achieved which you are pleased with. What did you have to do to achieve it?

- Think of one real event which has made you happy, and another which made you unhappy, or which really wound you up. They may be small things, which happened recently, or things which stick in your mind from a while ago; they may have happened to you or to someone close to you.

Then ask the young people to get into small groups and discuss the answers that they have written down.
If it seems tricky to get the conversation going, try offering some examples and asking whether the young people have experienced something similar. The answers to this section could be as simple as getting to the next level on a game (making them happy) or their teacher telling them off for something they didn't do (making them wound up), the death of a pet (making them sad).

> **TIP** "It often helps to allow the young people to discuss their responses in pairs before sharing them with the group."

Next encourage them to share their answers and thoughts with the whole group.
Encourage each small group to share their responses with the whole group unless you have an enormous group in which case stick with small groups or it will take for ever!

What did they write down? Why? As you begin this conversation ask someone to write down the responses on the flip chart so that everyone can see. Are there any issues you can explore further? If there are take a few minutes to look at them in more depth:

- Why did these issues make you happy/unhappy?
- What happened?
- Who was involved?
- Who did it affect?
- How did they feel?

"Create your own life story!"

Split into small groups or pairs to do this exercise. Encourage the young people to be honest about what they really want in life. Once they have finished encourage some people to share their ideas, and write the answers down on a flip chart. Once you have filled your flip-chart page, stick it up on the wall. You will come back to them as part of the "Judge" section when we examine what God wants in our lives.

There is space in their journal for them to write their responses to these questions.

Ask the young people:
If you could write your own life story, where would you be in five years' time, ten years' time and when you are 65 years old? *Write these answers down.*

To get the conversation going you might give them some ideas:

- **5 years** – in work or at university?
- **10 years** – married or single? What possessions do you think you might have? House? Car?
- **65 years old** – grandchildren? Retired or working?

> **TIP** " In this book all text with a yellow bar beside it is also printed in the candidates' journals. "

JUDGE

*Choose **two** or more of the four sections below. If you have lots of time or you want to add in an extra session you could do all the options. All the options are available in their journal. Alternatively you could encourage the young people to do further work on it at home during the week if they are interested and motivated.*

A: Gospel enquiry

Invite the group to listen carefully to the story and to think about the time, place and people involved. Perhaps you could ask a member of the group to read.

Read the Gospel, Luke 15:1-6

"The tax collectors and the sinners were all seeking the company of Jesus to hear what he had to say, and the Pharisees and the scribes complained. 'This man,' they said, 'welcomes sinners and eats with them.' So he spoke this parable to them: 'What man among you with a hundred sheep, losing one, would not leave the ninety-nine in the wilderness and go after the missing one till he found it? And when he found it, would he not joyfully take it on his shoulders and then, when he got home, call together his friends and neighbours? 'Rejoice with me,' he would say, 'I have found my sheep that was lost.'"

And discuss together…
- Who is in this story?
- What happened?
- What was said?
- How do you think the people present would have reacted to this? Why?
- Who do you think the lost sheep represents in this story? Who does the shepherd represent?
- What does this story say about how God views each one of us?
- What meaning does this story have for our lives?

Leader's ideas:

Repeat the story: a shepherd, leaving ninety-nine sheep on the hillside to go in search of just one, was risking losing his other sheep while he was away.

Tell the meaning: the meaning is that each one of us is special in God's eyes. We are told at the beginning of the Bible that we are made "in God's own image", and so we have a value that nothing in this world can take away. This is the message of the story: we are worth so much to God that God will search us out and care for us.

What does this mean in our lives? Put simply, God wants us to be happy and fulfilled. This is why Jesus also said, "I have come to give you life to the full." What does this say about our identity? That we are people who are loved by God!

B: What does our faith say?

QUOTE *"I have come so that they may have life and have it to the full."* From the Gospel of John

Leader reads aloud:
Our faith says that anything that is good, and all love, is from God. This is how God wants us to be happy: to strive for goodness and to always love.

And discuss together…
- Is this realistic?
- How many of your answers to what Jesus wants for us agree with your answers during the "See" section about what you think will make you happy in life?

C: God's life story for you…

Ask the young people to consider what they think God wants for them in five years' time, ten years' time and when they are 65 years old.

Write these answers down on a flip-chart page and stick it beside the flip chart full of their own aspirations.

Then discuss whether there are any differences between what they wrote down that they wanted in the earlier exercise and what they think God wants for them, and explore why this might be.

Things you might want to explore: What are the things society teaches us to desire (e.g. wealth, fame, possessions, success, etc.)? Are these the things we actually want and will make us happy? What are the things that God finds valuable in life (e.g. caring for others, loving, being in a community, being the best person we can be, etc.)? Try to tease out of the young people what Jesus stood for: Love, peace, justice, forgiveness, joy, righteousness, etc. Jesus came to show us to serve one another. Being a Christian is more than about being nice, it's about being good. What do you think this means? What is the difference between being nice and being good?

D: A sacramental sign

If your parish priest is happy for you to do so, show the pot containing the oil of chrism to the young people so that they can see what the oil of chrism looks like.

Tell the group:
When you are confirmed you will be anointed with the oil of chrism. This is a special oil which was used at your baptism. It is a sign of your life in God.

Anointing in biblical times was a sign of abundance and joy. It marked you out as special.

Anointing is a way for God to show us that we are worth more than riches and that we will have fullness of life in God.

Ask the group:
- To think about what ways other people show you that you are valued.
- Are there any other ways that God shows you that you are valued and loved?

ACE

Meet

This section is intended to show the Catholic faith working in some people's lives. Each week there will be a profile of a young person and of someone who has been motivated by their faith to do something amazing. These texts are also in the young people's journal. You could mention them as something for the young people to read during the week, or you could make it the basis for a discussion in the whole group about living as a Christian.

Mwende

My name is Mwende. I came from Kenya two years ago. I'm still new to the country and I'm still learning new things. I enjoy being a Christian because it's something I like doing.

I serve in the church as an altar server, and it's something I do because I feel like I'm relaxed here. It's good for me because back home you don't have the opportunity to serve in the church, so being an altar server is a good honour for me.

I would like to be a nutritionist, and to help people know what's good for them and what's bad for them, and what they need to have in life to grow and prosper. An alternative to that: seeing young people happy makes me happy, so that encourages me to be a care worker, or someone who takes care of children.

José Antonio Abreu:

A Professor of Economics who is also a government minister doesn't really sound like the kind of person to start a youth movement. But that is what José Antonio Abreu has done. He turned his Catholic faith into action. After a distinguished academic career and time spent as the culture minister for the government in his native Venezuela, José Antonio Abreu founded an organisation called El Sistema (The System). It brought classical music lessons to children in the slums. These children were often not in school and many were involved in crime. The capital city, Caracas, is one of the most violent places in the world. Many people thought his scheme would have no effect. They were wrong.

Today more than 400,000 people are involved in El Sistema. Giving children in slums music lessons doesn't just give them the chance to play music, it widens their horizons, gives them a sense of achievement and teaches them skills. All around the world Venezuelan slum kids are getting jobs with top orchestras. One of these is Edicson Ruiz. When he was eleven he was given lessons on the double bass. He said having music in his life saved him: "When I woke up in the morning I didn't know if I would have any food to eat but I knew I could play music and feed my soul." Today he plays with the Berlin Philharmonic Orchestra, one of the best orchestras in the world.

QUOTE

"Let us reveal to our children the beauty of music and music shall reveal to our children the beauty of life." *José Antonio Abreu*

Deciding on your action

So far we have looked at hopes and aspirations in life, and what causes sadness and happiness. We have thought about what our faith has to tell us about this. When we look at how our real lives and faith combine, it leads to action. Once we have thought through God's perspective on our lives, we are ready to decide on an action.

Personal action:
Encourage the young people to commit to doing something during the next week which will help bring God's goodness and love to someone else. Ideally this should be as a result of their own notes about **real life** *and* **faith**. *The action can be very small and hidden if they want. They can write the action down in their journal but they do not need to share it with the group at all.*

To get their ideas started you could make some suggestions or ask some questions. Perhaps suggest doing something for someone in their family or being kind to someone at school. Or ask questions such as "Can you think of anyone who would welcome a helping hand?"

Tell the young people that at each session they will be asked if they have done their action and whether they want to share their experience with the group. Remind them that they do not have to share or tell anyone about their action if they do not want to.

Let's look back at the notes we made at the beginning. Think again about the areas of our lives we said have made us unhappy.

- Is there anything we can do to change that situation?
- Can we help others that may be in that situation too?

Group action:
- What can we pray about?

Ask everyone to write a very simple intention (e.g. "for victims of bullying", "for my little sister who is ill", etc.) on a small piece of paper. These will be used during the closing prayer.

> **TIP** "If the young people are planning a service project for after confirmation, there may be things they've noticed in today's discussion which they could help do something about."

Before you begin the closing prayer section, encourage the young people to read through and fill in their journal during the week ahead. Remind them that it is a tool to help them on their journey to confirmation. Their journal contains lots more information and ideas than can be covered in each section.

QUOTE "This is my commandment: love one another, as I have loved you." *From the Gospel of John*

PRAYER

You will need the candle and a basket or bowl for prayer intentions.

This short prayer and meditation can be done in church with candles lit and lights dimmed. Perhaps you could all gather on the sanctuary, sitting on the floor in front of the altar. If using the church isn't practical you could instead sit in a circle around the candle as at the beginning of the session. You can use all the prayer and meditation below or just the prayer if you prefer. You might find it helpful to have meditative music in the background and perhaps an image – whether a photo, a statue, an ikon or a Bible – beside the candle and basket to act as a prayer focus.

Ask the young people to put their prayer intentions in the basket. They don't need to tell anyone what they have written. Invite the group to become still. Light the prayer candle again.

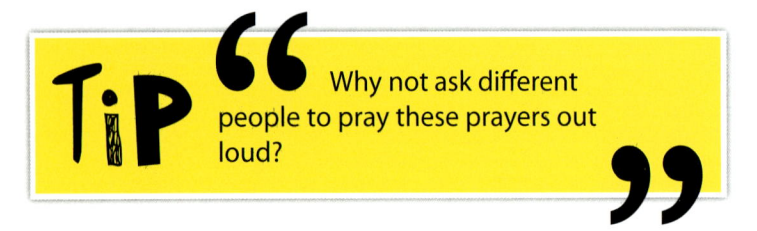

> **TIP:** Why not ask different people to pray these prayers out loud?

Read the following excerpt from Psalm 139

This is a reading from one of the ancient psalms in the Bible. It reminds us that we are all special to God:

Lord, you examine me and know me,
You know when I sit, when I rise,
You understand my thoughts from afar.
You watch when I walk or lie down,
You know every detail of my conduct.

A word is not yet on my tongue
Before you, Lord, know all about it.
You fence me in, behind and in front,
You have laid your hand upon me.
Such amazing knowledge is beyond me,
A height to which I cannot attain.

You created my inmost self,
Knit me together in my mother's womb.
For so many marvels I thank you;
A wonder am I, and all your works are wonders.

Final Prayer

Thank you, Lord,
for loving us into existence.
Thank you for helping us to understand the world around us
and for inspiring us to change it for the better.
Protect us, Lord, as we follow you through this week.
Strengthen us in our quest for happiness for ourselves
and for all our friends.
Amen.

As you end the session, remind the candidates of the date and time of the next session.

SESSION 2

Baptism — winning the lottery

Session 2
Baptism – winning the Lottery

Aim:
To help the young people to understand our reality as Christians: claimed by God and with a special task in life, to be part of the Church community.

Leader's reflection:
Do you ever think about why you are a Christian? Have you always been a Christian? Have there been times when you wish you weren't a Christian? Perhaps you have seen people who claim to be Christian behaving or speaking in a way which you do not want to be associated with? What makes you proud to be a Christian? Who are your inspirations in the Church?

However we may have come to membership of the Church, we have the great privilege of being part of a global community of those who believe in Christ and who choose to put Christ at the centre of their identity. This session helps the young people understand their membership of the Church, which they joined when they were baptised.

> **TIP** If there is a team of catechists in your parish, perhaps you could meet together for a few minutes before every session and read and think through the leader's reflection each week?

You will need:
- A candle and something to light it with
- Some relaxing/meditative music
- Flip-chart paper and pens
- Small pieces of paper for the young people to write their prayer intentions on and some pens/pencils to write with
- A basket or something to place the prayer intentions in at the end of the session

Candidates will need:
- Their candidate journal and a pen

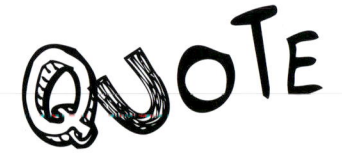

QUOTE "Peter answered… 'every one of you must be baptised in the name of Jesus Christ for the forgiveness of your sins, and you will receive the gift of the Holy Spirit.'" *From the Acts of the Apostles*

Begin with a prayer…

As the young people begin to arrive have the lights in the room dimmed, a candle lit in the centre. As each person arrives, invite them to sit quietly in a circle around the candle. Perhaps play some reflective music in the background.

> Loving Lord Jesus,
> when you were baptised you showed the world that you were one with God our Father. Thank you for giving us the gift of baptism, making each one of us a part of your family in the Church. Through our session today may we come to a greater understanding of you, so that we may grow as Christians in your love.
> Amen.

TiP " This prayer is also printed in the candidates' books. Perhaps ask one of the young people to pray it out loud while everyone adopts a posture of their choice, conducive to prayer. "

To get us started…

This is a good time to mention any "housekeeping" items: welcome anyone who was not able to make the first session, introduce them to the group, etc.

To get everyone started, begin with a group exercise to help everyone feel comfortable in each other's company. Use the following activity, or another one of your choice.

- Start by getting the young people into small groups of 6-10 people. If there is room have them lie down in a line in their group. You can do this sitting down on chairs in a line if there isn't room to lie down.

- Once they are all lying or sitting in their groups ask the first person in the line to say "Ha", then the next person to say "Ha, Ha", then the next person to say "Ha, Ha, Ha" and so on, building up the number of "Ha, Ha, Ha"s.

- When you get to the end of the line, start at the beginning adding even more "ha"s. It is guaranteed to descend into giggling as people struggle to get the right number of "ha"s or just become aware of the silliness of the exercise

- This doesn't need to be a long exercise: once everyone is laughing, get everyone back to their seats.

Once the laughter has died down and everyone is back in their seats tell the group the point of the exercise:

You were acting as a group, taking on a role (to pass on the right number of "ha"s) and having fun. In today's session we will look at another group you are all part of – the worldwide Christian community of the Church. We will also be looking at your role in that group.

SEE

In this section we encourage the young people to examine the things that happen to them in their lives.

"What does being a Christian mean to you?"

What groups do the young people in your session today belong to? Are they sporty? Or in a music group? Are they involved in their local community or do they have a hobby that they share with other people who are interested in the same things? Encourage the young people to think about their lives: the groups that they belong to, the things they like about this, and what they expect from their groups. Read aloud the following questions and discuss them in the group. We'll return to them in the "Act" section as a basis for thinking about what action we could take this week.

> **TIP** " It often helps to allow the young people to discuss their responses in pairs before sharing them with the group. "

Ask the whole group to think on their own and to write in their journal.

- Write down three things that you do because you are a Christian.
- Write down three things that make it hard to be a Christian.

Encourage them to share their answers in small groups and to think about why they chose those answers. You can challenge the group by asking them further questions to consider:

- Why do you have to be a Christian to do that?
- How does a Christian do that differently? Why is that hard?
- Can you think of a specific situation or event when being a Christian has been hard?

What did they write down? Why? As you begin this conversation ask someone to write down the responses on the flip chart so that everyone can see. Are there any issues you can explore further? If there are, take a few minutes to look at them in more depth:

- What happened?
- Who was involved?
- Why was this difficult?
- Can you think of any alternatives to what happened?

Belonging to a group

Say to the young people:
We are thinking today a little about what it means to be a Christian. Baptism is the moment when we were welcomed into the Christian Church or "group". Now we will spend some time thinking about what it means to be part of any group.

Ask them the following questions to discuss in their small groups.

- What groups do you belong to?
  (You can make some suggestions – sports teams, school clubs, an orchestra, Scouts, Guides, social networks, your friendship groups, etc.)

- What do these groups expect from you?
  (e.g. following the rules, turning up to practices, etc.)

- What do you expect from them?
  (e.g. fun, friendship, a sense of achievement, etc.)

Leader's note:
If they are struggling to come up with many groups themselves, these questions can be broadened to the less formal groupings in young people's lives. For example: What kind of music do you listen to? Do you follow the fashions of a particular group? Are you a fan of a particular person, book, film or TV programme that helps to define you? Can you tell by looking at some people what kind of music they like? How can you identify them?

Ask the young people to think about what the signs are of belonging to any of the groups they have flagged up (e.g. uniform or team strip, places you meet, people you hang around with, kinds of clothes you choose, etc.)

Write these down on a flip chart.

Remind the young people that these are all signs of belonging to a group and that as Christians we have special ways of marking out our belonging to the Church.

JUDGE

*Do at least **two** of the three sections below. All the options are available in the young people's journals so if you don't do all the sections you could encourage the young people to do further work on it at home during the week if they are interested and motivated.*

A: Gospel enquiry

Invite the group to listen carefully to the story and to think about the time, place and people involved. Perhaps you could ask a member of the group to read. The Gospel text is printed in their journals.

Read the Gospel, Matthew 3:13-17

"Jesus came from Galilee to the Jordan to be baptised by John. John tried to dissuade him, with the words, 'It is I who need baptism from you, and yet you come to me!' But Jesus replied, 'Leave it like this for the time being; it is fitting that we should, in this way, do all that uprightness demands.' Then John gave in to him. And when Jesus had been baptised he at once came up from the water, and suddenly the heavens opened and he saw the Spirit of God descending like a dove and coming down on him. And suddenly there was a voice from heaven, 'This is my Son, the Beloved; my favour rests on him.'"

And discuss together…
- Who is in this story?
- What happened?
- What was said?
- How do you think the people present would have reacted to this? Why?
- What does this story say about our baptism?

When Jesus was baptised two very important things happened:
1. The Holy Spirit descended upon Jesus.
2. God the Father revealed Jesus as his "beloved Son".

It may help to imagine winning the lottery! When we win the lottery we've won the moment our numbers come up, but we still need to go and claim our prize money. When we were conceived and God gave us life, we won the lottery. We are made a child of God. Our baptism is the moment we claim the prize. We claim the fact that we are children of God and receive our prize – the gift of the Holy Spirit to help us to live like true lottery winners!

Ask the young people what they think of this idea. Do they find it helpful?
Can you think of how baptism differs from winning the lottery?

Leader's note:
Explore the fact that the lottery has few winners but everyone is a child of God and millions of people get baptised. With God we can all be winners!

B: What does our faith say?

QUOTE *"What marks us in the eyes of our enemies is our loving kindness. 'Only look,' they say, 'look how they love one another.'"* An ancient Christian philosopher called Tertullian wrote this down in the second century AD to explain what Roman citizens made of Christians at the time.

Leader reads aloud:
At baptism we are "reborn" as children of God. We belong to God's family. Baptism is our initiation ceremony into the family of God.

When we receive the gift of the Holy Spirit, it involves an obligation to respond to that gift. From the moment we are baptised we are meant to live our lives for God, continuing the work of Jesus in the world. As Christians, we should live differently and people should know who we are.

Ask the group to discuss what marks them out as Christians:
- What marks you out as a Christian?
- How can people around us know that we are Christian?
- What does being Christian mean in our daily lives?

QUOTE *"Jesus said, 'John baptised with water but, not many days from now, you are going to be baptised with the Holy Spirit.'"* From the Acts of the Apostles

C: A sacramental sign

If your parish priest is happy for you to do so, perhaps you could gather round the font in church for this part. You could even set it up as though for a baptism.

Tell the group: When you were baptised there were two main signs: **water** and **oil**.

Ask them what they think the water might symbolise.
Suggested answers: *It is a drink; we use it for washing; we cannot live without it.*

You could tell the group that baptism used to be done by completely dunking you in a river or large pool – this is called complete immersion. As we come up out of the water, we come into a new life with God. We belong to God now, not the world.

Ask them why they think these two symbols are used in baptism.
Suggested answers: *The water from the font symbolises our old life being washed away as we become one of God's children. The oil shows that we are important, loved, chosen and cherished by God.*

Say to the group: **We are preparing for the sacrament of confirmation when we will repeat for ourselves the promises made at our baptism. The gifts we receive at confirmation will help us to fulfil these promises.**

You could direct the young people to their journal which contains the texts of the promises made at their baptism. Perhaps they could read them through during the week ahead?

ACE

This section is intended to show the Catholic faith working in some people's lives. Each week there will be a profile of a young person and of someone who has been motivated by their faith to do something amazing. These texts are also in the young people's journal. You could mention them as something for the young people to read during the week or you could make it the basis for a discussion in the whole group to enable each individual and the whole group to decide how they are going to take action.

Meet

Michael

My Catholic faith has a place in every aspect of my life. And so, even if I don't take everything to heart every single second of my life, it does create certain guidelines and certain values that I've taken as my own, which help me to make better decisions.

Overall, I think faith is something personal, that you look to find comfort and guidance from. There are 1.2 billion Catholics worldwide, 1.2 billion different interpretations of the faith. But it's just one faith, and there are core things that draw us in together to be Catholic: we believe in God, we believe in the life of Jesus.

But I think there are lots of rules that we have to question so that our faith can sit right with us. And it's only through questioning things that we get to the truth.

Frank Cottrell Boyce

I'm a Catholic and I write movies. Faith and cinema have always been connected in my mind, partly because when I was little I used sometimes to go to a church in a converted cinema – it still had velvety flip seats instead of pews, and a big screen behind the altar.

My first job was writing soap opera (*Coronation Street*). I loved it, but in the end I knew other people could write it just as well – or better – than I could. Whatever you do creatively, in the end, you have to find the thing that only you can do, the thing that uses all of you.

So I started to write my faith in a lot more. I wrote a film called *Millions* – which is about a little boy whose Mum has died and who sees saints. A lot of people thought that seeing saints was a sign of mental disturbance, whereas I thought it was a blessing. Fortunately I had a great director, Danny Boyle, on my side and he stood up for me. I was worried that sticking so strongly to a Catholic point of view would alienate people, but it's had the opposite effect.

As a Catholic I have a common bond with millions of other Catholics all over the world. Cinema is just the same. It tries to find stories that work for everyone, all over the world. It tries to strike that common chord. A lot of people find that really hard to do but as a Catholic it's just part of how I think. We are all sons and daughters of God, and all brothers and sisters in the Spirit of Christ – a great family.

QUOTE

"I think people can sense that you're putting all of yourself into something and they respect that."
Frank Cottrell Boyce

Frank Cottrell Boyce is a patron of Missio, which helps to share faith and connect people and churches throughout the world. For more information see www.missio.org.uk

Deciding on your action

So far we have looked at how we have been made part of the Church community through our baptism and at how we all belong to different groups. We have also thought about what happened at baptism both for Jesus at his baptism and for us when we were baptised.

When we look at how our real lives and faith combine, it leads to action. Once we have thought through God's perspective on our lives we are ready to decide on an action.

Personal action:
Ask the young people whether they did do the action they decided on at last week's session. Remind them that it isn't too late if they haven't. They can always do it this week alongside their next action.

Ask the young people how they found doing their action.

Tell the group:
Today we have looked at what it means to belong to a group and what it means to be Christian. There should be something different about us, because we are baptised and chosen by God for this specific task. There are some areas of our life, which we spoke of, where it is hard to be a Christian.

Is there anything you can do in these areas of difficulty to try and live as Christians?

Encourage the young people to commit to doing something during the next week in which they will act as a Christian in a way that they find difficult. Ideally this should be as a result of their own notes about real life and faith. The action can be very small and hidden if they want. They can write the action down in their journal but they do not need to share it with the group at all.

To get their ideas started you could make some suggestions or ask some questions. Perhaps suggest trying to include someone they would normally try to avoid at school. Or not doing something they know is wrong even though other people are doing it. Or ask questions such as "Can you think of a time this week when you can show someone that you recognise that they are valued?"

Tell the young people that at each session they will be asked if they have done their action and whether they want to share their experience with the group. Remind them that they do not have to share or tell anyone about their action if they do not want to.

Choosing a confirmation name and sponsor
Tell the group that at their confirmation they will choose a new name for themselves: this will be their confirmation name. They can choose any name so long as there is a saint that shares this name. Because they may want some time to think about what name they will choose, one of their personal actions over the coming weeks can be to think about what name they would like and to find out something about the saint who shares that name.

Each candidate will also need to choose a sponsor, an adult confirmed Catholic who will stand beside them at the moment they receive the Holy Spirit in confirmation and who will be willing to act as a Christian guide throughout life. Ask the young people in the group to begin thinking about who would be an appropriate sponsor. They could make a list and then approach their preferred person to see if they would be willing to take on the role.

Group action:
Is there anything we can do as a group to take action on what you have been discussing today?

What can we pray about?
You can encourage the young people to see praying as one way of taking action as a group.

Ask everyone to write a very simple intention (e.g. "for victims of bullying", "for my little sister who is ill", etc.) on a small piece of paper. These will be used during the closing prayer.

> **TIP** " If the young people are planning a service project, there may be things they've noticed in today's discussion which they could help do something about. "

Before you begin the closing prayer section, encourage the young people to read through and fill in their journal during the week ahead. Remind them that it is a tool to help them on their journey to confirmation. Their journal contains lots more information and ideas than can be covered in each section.

QUOTE **"You must see what great love the Father has lavished on us by letting us be called God's children – which is what we are!"**
From the first letter of St John

PRAYER

You will need the candle and a basket or bowl for the prayer intentions.

This short prayer and meditation can be done in church with candles lit and lights dimmed. Perhaps you could all gather in church, sitting on the floor close to the altar. If using the church isn't practical you could instead sit in a circle around the candle as at the beginning of the session. You can use all the prayer and meditation below or just the prayer if you prefer. You might find it helpful to have meditative music in the background and perhaps an image – whether a photo, a statue, an icon or a Bible – beside the candle and basket to act as a prayer focus.

Ask the young people to put their prayer intentions in the basket. They don't need to tell anyone what they have written. Invite the group to become still. Light the prayer candle again.

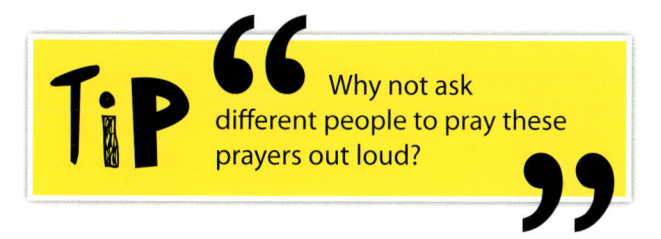

> **TIP** " Why not ask different people to pray these prayers out loud? "

Loving God, we bring before you our concerns and our hopes. We thank you for making us your children. May we travel towards the sacrament of confirmation confident in your love, knowing that you will grant us the strength to follow you even when it is difficult to stay faithful to your ways. Amen.

Silence for a short while.

Read the following excerpt from St Paul's letter to the Romans (8:14-17)

This is a reading from a letter which St Paul wrote to the Christian community living in Rome. They were being persecuted by the Romans for their faith and Paul wrote to encourage them to stay faithful to Jesus:

"All who are guided by the Spirit of God are children of God; for what you received was not the spirit of slavery to bring you back into fear; you received the Spirit of adoption, enabling us to cry out 'Abba, Father!' The Spirit himself joins with our spirit to bear witness that we are children of God. And if we are children, then we are heirs, heirs of God and joint-heirs with Christ."

Final Prayer

Thank you, Lord,
for welcoming us into your family,
the Church.
Through your love for us we will grow
and become the
people you intend us to be.
May we come closer to you as we go
through this week
and for the rest of our lives.
Amen.

As you end the session, remind the candidates of the date and time of the next session.

Session 3

Confirmation – Confirming our Role

Session 3
Confirmation – Confirming our Role

Aim:
To understand what really happens at confirmation and the responsibility that each candidate must take on, as individuals and as part of the Church community.

Leader's reflection:
Can you remember the day of your confirmation? How did you feel? What did you think was going to happen?

When you were confirmed did it live up to your expectations? Did you feel different?
What do you think the young people in your group are feeling about their confirmation day? What can you do to help them understand what they are preparing for? Is there anything that your parish do to make sure that each young person can have a role in the church community after they are confirmed? How can you support them to take action in the wider community?

> **TIP:** If there is a team of catechists in your parish, perhaps you could meet together for a few minutes before every session and read and think through the leader's reflection each week?

You will need:
- A candle and something to light it with
- Some relaxing/meditative music
- Flip-chart paper and pens
- Small pieces of paper for the young people to write their prayer intentions on and some pens/pencils to write with
- A basket or something to place the prayer intentions in at the end of the session

Candidates will need:
- Their candidate journal and a pen

QUOTE "Now Christ's body is yourselves, each of you with a part to play in the whole."
From the first letter St Paul sent to the Corinthians

Begin with a prayer…

As the young people begin to arrive have the lights in the room dimmed, a candle lit in the centre. As each person arrives, invite them to sit quietly in a circle around the candle. Perhaps play some reflective music in the background.

> Dear Lord, we gather again today to hear your word and to learn more about you. Thank you for your presence among us here, now and always. As we prepare for our confirmation we ask that we may be guided by your Holy Spirit so that we may listen, understand and grow in the light of your love. Amen.

TIP " This prayer is also printed in the candidates' books. Perhaps ask one of the young people to pray it out loud while everyone adopts a posture of their choice, conducive to prayer. "

To get us started…

By this session all the candidates should know one another and should know who you are. This activity aims to get them to know each other on a deeper level.

If I were a…
Ask each person to think of answers, with reasons, to the following questions:

If I were a fictional character I would be…   because…

If I were an animal I would be a…   because…

If I were a kind of food I would be a…   because…

You can give them some examples:
If I were a fictional character I would be Speedy Gonzalez because I'm always rushing around.
If I were an animal I would be a cat because I love to sleep.
If I were a kind of food I would be chocolate because I'm sweet and tasty.

If they want to they can write their answers in their journal before sharing them with the group.

TIP " If you want to make this exercise longer, ask the group to think up new questions or discuss whether the answers really have meaning in helping us to get to know one another. "

SEE

In this section we encourage the young people to examine the things that happen to them in their lives and the lives of those around them.

"Why are you going to be confirmed?"

In this session try to encourage the young people to be honest about their motivation for being Confirmed. Try also to tease out all the possible reasons for being confirmed.

Ask the young people to think on their own and to write in their journal

- Write down what you think is the main reason you have decided to be confirmed.
- Has anyone influenced your decision?

Remind the group that it doesn't matter what their reason is for coming forward to be confirmed. Being honest about it is an important part of the process.

Try offering some examples to show them how honest they are allowed to be! "I'm doing it to make my Mum happy"; "I'm doing it because there will be a party afterwards and I like being the centre of attention"; right through to "I'm doing it because I want to commit myself to my faith."

Then ask the young people to get into pairs and discuss the answers that they have written down

Next encourage them to share their answers and thoughts with the whole group

If you have a large group, break them into smaller groups for this.

What did they write down? Why?
As they share their reasons begin to write down their answers on a flip chart. See if the group will willingly discuss the different reasons, and why they think there are different reasons for being confirmed.

Read aloud:
Through the gifts of the Holy Spirit we receive at confirmation we get direct help from God to live out the task God gave us at baptism. All through our lives we all want to be independent but we are all in need of help sometimes.

Ask the young people to:

- Name something that they have needed help with recently. It doesn't matter how large or small this is.
  This could be needing help to catch up on work they missed at school, or needing a lift to sports practice.

- Name one way in which they have responded to someone else's needs recently.
  This could be anything from taking a younger sibling to the park, to running errands for an elderly neighbour or just lending someone a pen at school.

- Can they identify any areas where they currently need help or can they think of someone they know who needs support?
  This could be needing some advice on a piece of schoolwork, or a classmate who we know is very stressed about upcoming exams.

Encourage the young people to write their answers down in their journal and then share them in pairs before sharing with the whole group.

Now ask the group to discuss the following two questions
- What do you think the word "faith" means?
- Is it important to be confirmed into the Catholic faith?

Depending on how well your group are working together you could do this as a large group or in pairs or small groups. It might help to keep the discussion on track to have the questions written down on a flip chart.

JUDGE

*Choose at least **two** of the three sections below. If you have lots of time or you want to add in an extra session you could do all the options. All the options are available in the candidates' journals. Alternatively you could encourage the young people to do further work on it at home during the week if they are interested and motivated.*

A: Scripture enquiry

Invite the group to listen carefully to the story and to think about the time, place and people involved. Perhaps you could ask a member of the group to read. The text is printed in their journals.

Read Acts 2:1-4

"When Pentecost day came round, they had all met together, when suddenly there came from heaven a sound as of a violent wind which filled the entire house in which they were sitting; and there appeared to them tongues as of fire; these separated and came to rest on the head of each of them. They were all filled with the Holy Spirit and began to speak different languages as the Spirit gave them power to express themselves."

And discuss together…

- Who is in this story? (Ask them to also think about who is not in this story – Jesus has gone to heaven and left his apostles seemingly alone.)
- What happened?
- What was said?
- How do you think the people present reacted to this? Why?
- How do you think you might have reacted if you had been there?
- What does this story tell us about what Jesus has done to support his followers?

Leader's ideas:
Repeat the story with a little background: after Jesus went up to heaven his apostles were all frightened – they were alone without their leader and they also risked being persecuted by the Jewish authorities for being friends with Jesus. They gather in a room when suddenly a great wind and tongues of fire appear from heaven. This is God's sign that they are receiving the gift of the Holy Spirit. This Spirit allows them to do amazing things including speaking in different languages.

Tell the meaning: *Jesus sent his Holy Spirit to be with his apostles to give them strength and courage to face the difficult times ahead. We hear that they were given the power to "express themselves". They were given all the help they needed.*

This happens at our confirmation. We are confirmed as baptised people who have a job to do. The Church confirms us and says to us: "You have a unique role to play, without you the Church is not complete." The gift of the Holy Spirit empowers us to fulfil our role, to express ourselves, in the Church and in the world.

If you want to and there is time you could:
- Ask the young people what they think of this.
- Ask them in what way they think they might be called to "express themselves".

40

B: What does our faith say?

When you are confirmed you will receive the seven gifts of the Holy Spirit.

What are they?
You could ask the group to guess (but the answer is in their journal so make sure they have their books closed and haven't read ahead!) and write their suggestions on a flip chart. Circle any correct ones (including those that mean roughly the same thing even if they aren't the exact words) as you go along.

1. Wisdom
2. Understanding
3. Right Judgement (also sometimes called "counsel")
4. Courage (also sometimes called "fortitude")
5. Knowledge
6. Reverence (also sometimes called "piety")
7. Awe of God (also sometimes called "fear of God")

Ask the group what they think each one means. There are some suggested answers below but your group might come up with better ones!

Wisdom: *Applying knowledge and experience together well.*

Understanding: *Seeing through the eyes of Jesus by using love to give us insight into things.*

Right Judgement: *Making the right choices in life.*

Courage: *Being ready to do what we think is right even though we find it difficult.*

Knowledge: *Coming to know God as much as we can.*

Reverence: *Appreciating all the wonderful things God does for us, from the largest (sending his son Jesus to die on the cross for us) to the smallest (a flower, a sunset, etc.)*

Awe of God: *Accepting that God is greater than we can ever understand.*

Ask the group to think of situations when they could put these gifts into practice. Encourage them to look back at their answers in the "See" section and think about when they needed help:
- *At home*
- *At school*
- *In the parish*
- *With friends*

Ask the group whether they think these gifts will help them to "express themselves".

41

C: A sacramental sign

If you can, show the group a picture of the bishop laying his hands on a young person at a confirmation. A picture is provided opposite but if you had one from your own parish that might be even better.

> **Tell the group:** Our faith tells us that at Confirmation our baptism is confirmed and that we are sealed with the gift of the Holy Spirit.
>
> **There are two main signs used at confirmation:**
> - The laying on of hands
> - And the anointing with the oil of chrism.

Ask the young people to discuss what they think the laying on of hands symbolises.
Suggested answer: it is the sign of the giving and receiving of the Holy Spirit.

The oil of chrism was used at your baptism. What does it symbolise?
Suggested answer: Anointing with oil comes from the idea of anointing kings, warriors and athletes with oil in ancient times, to give them strength in the struggles and challenges ahead.

At your confirmation, it will be a symbol that you are strengthened by the Holy Spirit.

Ask the young people why they think these signs are used particularly for confirmation.
Suggested answer: confirmation is when we receive the gifts of the Holy Spirit and when we fully accept our role as Christians.

43

ACE

This section is intended to show the Catholic faith working in some people's lives. Each week there will be a profile of a young person and of someone who has been motivated by their faith to do something amazing. These texts are also in the young people's journal. You could mention them as something for the young people to read during the week or you could make it the basis for a discussion in the whole group about living as a Christian.

Meet

John Jo

I'm John Jo and I'm fifteen. What I think it means to be a Catholic is showing your love and appreciation for what God has given you in everyday life.

I took up charity work with the national society for epilepsy because my sister was diagnosed with epilepsy a few years ago. And I've had to deal with the traumatic times when she's had a fit and I've been on my own. I've had to grow up in that situation and learn some of the horrible truths of life. I think it shouldn't have to be that horrible for someone else of my age. And I think I could make that happen with charity work.

In my school I organized an own clothes day single handedly and we raised £2,000 for this, and the charity were very grateful.

Jean Vanier

Born into an important Canadian political family, Jean Vanier's parents might have expected him to become a leader of some sort and so he did – but probably not in a way they envisaged. He was born in 1928 and after serving in the Navy following the Second World War he became a theologian. Whilst teaching philosophy in France he met two men, Raphael Simi and Philippe Seux. They both had developmental disabilities and were living in a large institution. Jean Vanier felt God's call and invited the men to share a home with him. He called this "L'Arche", the Ark. This became the first of many communities worldwide where people with developmental disabilities live in a family-like setting with those who come to assist them. There are ten L'Arche communities in the UK and almost 150 worldwide. Jean Vanier didn't just recognise that God loves everybody and that everybody has great value. He showed it by improving the lives of many people marginalised by their disabilities.

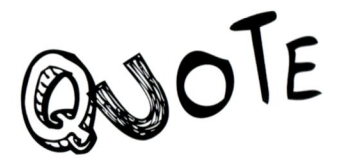

QUOTE

"Love doesn't mean doing extraordinary or heroic things. It means knowing how to do ordinary things with tenderness." *Jean Vanier*

"Every child, every person needs to know that they are a source of joy; every child, every person, needs to be celebrated. Only when all of our weaknesses are accepted as part of our humanity can our negative, broken self-images be transformed." *Jean Vanier*

For more information on the L'Arche communities visit www.larche.org and for more information on Jean Vanier visit www.jean-vanier.org

Deciding on your action

So far today we have thought about how we all need help sometimes and about the role our faith can play in providing some of that help. When we look at how our real lives and faith combine, it leads to action. Once we have thought through God's perspective on our lives we are ready to decide on an action.

Personal action:
Encourage the young people to commit to doing something during the next week which will help bring God's goodness and love to someone else. Ideally this should be as a result of their own notes about real life and faith. The action can be very small and hidden if they want. They can write the action down in their journal but they do not need to share it with the group at all.

To get their ideas started you could make some suggestions or ask some questions. Perhaps suggest doing something for someone in their family or being kind to someone at school. Or ask questions such as "Can you think of anyone who might welcome your help this week?"

Tell the young people that at each session they will be asked if they have done their action and whether they want to share their experience with the group. Remind them that they do not have to share or tell anyone about their action if they do not want to.

Let's look back at the notes we made at the beginning. Think again about the areas of our lives where we said we needed help and areas where we have given help. Remember the gifts of the Holy Spirit.

How have you suggested the gifts of the Holy Spirit can be used in your life?
Does thinking about the gifts of the Holy Spirit help you to think about what you can do this week?

Group action:
Is there anything we can do as a group to take action on what you have been discussing today?

> **TIP** "If your parish is supportive you could organise a helpful job for the young people to do within the parish – perhaps tidying up the benches after Mass, or handing out the hymn books before Mass, or taking up the offertory. Or is there a local community action project you could encourage people to consider?"

What can we pray about?

You can encourage the young people to see praying as one way of taking action as a group.

Ask everyone to write a very simple intention (e.g. "for victims of bullying", "for my little sister who is ill", etc.) on a small piece of paper. These will be used during the closing prayer. By now the group may know each other well enough to share their intentions aloud. You can ask the group if anyone feels ready, but be clear that there is no pressure and that they never need to share it with anyone but God unless they want to.

TIP "If the young people are planning a service project for after confirmation, there may be things they've noticed in today's discussion which they could help do something about."

Before you begin the closing prayer section, encourage the young people to read through and fill in their journal during the week ahead. Remind them that it is a tool to help them on their journey to confirmation. Their journal contains lots more information and ideas than can be covered in each section.

QUOTE "Ask, and it will be given to you; search, and you will find; knock, and the door will be opened to you."
From the Gospel of St Matthew

PRAYER

You will need the candle and a basket or bowl for prayer intentions.

This short prayer and meditation can be done in church with candles lit and lights dimmed. Perhaps you could all gather on the sanctuary, sitting on the floor in front of the altar. If using the church isn't practical you could instead sit in a circle around the candle as at the beginning of the session. You can use all the prayer and meditation below or just the prayer if you prefer. You might find it helpful to have meditative music in the background and perhaps an image – whether a photo, a statue, an icon or a Bible – beside the candle and basket to act as a prayer focus.

Ask the young people to put their prayer intentions in the basket. They don't need to tell anyone what they have written. Invite the group to become still. Light the prayer candle again.

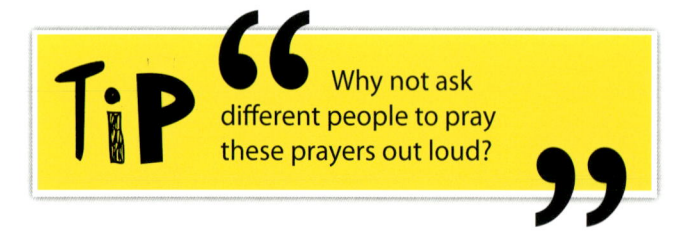

TIP "Why not ask different people to pray these prayers out loud?"

Lord, as we pray today we know that you will listen to these intentions we bring before you. We know that you will hear the desires of our hearts. May we, in return, hear your voice in our hearts as we pray.
Amen.

Silence for a short while.

Read the following prayer which was written by St Edmund of Abingdon in the 12th century.
Lord, since you exist, we exist. Since you are beautiful, we are beautiful.
Since you are good, we are good. By our existence we honour you.
By our beauty we glorify you. By our goodness we love you.
Lord, through your power all things were made.
Through your wisdom all things are governed. Through your grace all things are sustained.
Give us power to serve you,
wisdom to discern your laws and grace to obey those at all times.
Amen

Final Prayer
We thank you, Lord, for giving us life.
We thank you for the sending your Holy Spirit to live within our hearts.
We thank you for creating us with a purpose.
May we go out this week full of your love
so that we may share your saving help with others in the ways that we listen,
in the ways that we speak and in the acts that we do.
Amen.

> **TIP** "If you would like a longer prayer session why not use some of the prayers and bible readings in the candidates' journals?"

As you end the session, remind the candidates of the date and time of the next session.

SESSION 4

Getting it Right with God's Help

Session 4
Getting it Right with God's Help

Aim:
The aim of this session is to examine how we are called to try to live, if we are to follow Christ, and to examine how the sacraments are a help in life.

Leader's reflection:
Can you think of times in your life when you had difficult decisions to make? Who and what influenced you at these times? The young people in your group have so many difficult decisions ahead of them – when to leave school, what careers to pursue, who to build relationships with, and so many more. But it is not just the big, hard decisions we need help with. Every day we have choices about how to live. Being a Christian offers us a blueprint for how to live and how to discern between the many options our modern lives offer us. Today we will explore some aspects of this guidance Jesus has given us all.

> **TIP** If there is a team of catechists in your parish, perhaps you could meet together for a few minutes before every session and read and think through the leader's reflection each week?

You will need:
- Enough thin square mint chocolates (preferably a fair-trade equivalent to After Eights) for everyone to have at least one – it might be a good idea to have some spares in case they fall on the floor during the game.
- Baby wipes or kitchen roll for people to wipe their faces with after the game.
- A candle and something to light it with
- Some relaxing/meditative music
- Flip-chart paper and pens
- Small pieces of paper for the young people to write their prayer intentions on and some pens/pencils to write with
- A basket or something to place the prayer intentions in at the end of the session

Candidates will need:
- Their candidate journal and a pen

QUOTE *"The Lord is my shepherd… He guides me along the right path." From Psalm 23*

Begin with a prayer…

As the young people begin to arrive have the lights in the room dimmed, a candle lit in the centre. As each person arrives, invite them to sit quietly in a circle around the candle. Perhaps play some reflective music in the background.

> Dear Lord,
> We ask that you bless our time here together today. We ask that you will fill our hearts with your love and inspire us to listen to your words. We open our hearts to receive your goodness and love.
> Amen.

TIP: This prayer is also printed in the candidates' books. Perhaps you could ask one of the young people to pray it out loud.

To get us started…

This very silly game is guaranteed to be fun but makes a serious point.

The After Eight game
Split the group into small groups of three or four. It doesn't matter how many groups you have. Any adult helpers can join in too. Get every one to sit down on chairs in their groups. Ask one person in each group to start by putting the chocolate on their forehead with their head leaning back. Now ask them to move the chocolate into their mouth without using their hands – they will have to use their facial muscles and wiggle their heads to get the mint into their mouth. Tell them if it falls off they must put the mint back on their forehead and start again! Once the first person has successfully got the mint into their mouth, the next person has a go and so on.

Once they have all finished gather them into one big group. Ask them if they enjoyed the task and then tell them that it had a very serious point.

Getting a mint from your forehead to your mouth without using your hands is silly. It's not a good way to go about eating. Our hands are specially designed to help us. In a similar way trying to live our lives without God's help makes our lives unnecessarily difficult. We have someone to call on for help at all times – the Holy Spirit. Today we are going to look at how we, as Christians, are called to live our lives.

Christians don't do good things simply because they are born nice people. Doing the right thing takes work. Christians try to act in a certain way because Christ gave them the example of loving and gave them the Holy Spirit to help them to follow his example.

SEE

In this section we encourage the young people to examine the things that happen to them in their lives and the lives of those around them.

"What are you doing with your life?"

In this section try to get them to share things from their own lives.

Ask the young people to think on their own and to write in their journal

- What is one decision you have made which you are proud of?
- Can you think of a decision you made which went horribly wrong?

Try offering some examples from your own life as examples. Here are a few examples to get you thinking: "A good decision I made was going to a party one night when I didn't feel like going out because I met the man who is now my husband there." "A good decision was moving to my house because we have great neighbours." "A bad decision I made was to buy my current car. It keeps breaking down and I find it really uncomfortable to drive." "A bad decision I made was to change jobs from one I liked to one which paid better but I hated it."

Or you could offer examples which might reflect their lives: Are you proud of auditioning for the school play? Proud of being in the football team? Pleased that you decided to encourage your little sister to resolve a fight she was having with a friend?

Perhaps you feel you made the wrong decision when you dumped your girlfriend/boyfriend, or if you decided to give in to peer pressure to try smoking.

Then ask the young people to get into pairs and discuss the answers that they have written down

Encourage each pair to share their responses with the whole group. If you have a large group break them into smaller groups for this.

What did they write down? Why?

Say to the group:
> Today we are thinking about our own lives and how we choose to live them. Our choices, or decisions, are one of the most determining factors in our lives. Usually we make decisions based on our principles.

Ask the young people to discuss the following questions in pairs and then feed back to the group. If you have a large group you will need to split them into smaller groups for this feedback. There is space in their journals for them to write down their answers if they wish.

- What do you understand a principle to be?
- Name three principles you hope to live by as you grow as young adults in the world.

As they share their answers in the small groups, write down (or ask someone in each group to write down) their answers on a flip chart so everyone can see the answers.

Tell the group:
Sometimes our principles are referred to as our "moral code". We often hear this phrase on TV and in the media. People often pride themselves on having a moral code, and the media are always very quick to question other people's morals.

Ask the group: What do you think the Christian moral code is?

Write the answers down on a flip-chart. Here are some suggested ideas to get the conversation going if needed. Ideas could range from broad principles ("Christians believe that love should be at the centre of everything we do"; "Every human being is special because they are made in God's image so everything we do has to respect one another") to specific things ("It is wrong to kill another person"; "You shouldn't steal").

If you want to extend this section, once you have a lot of answers written on your chart you can ask the group to think about which of these things society as a whole follows and which it doesn't. This leads to the question – what is different about being a Christian? We will look at this in our "Judge" section.

QUOTE "It is not so essential to think much as to love much." *St Teresa of Jesus*

JUDGE

*Choose at least **two** of the three sections below. If you have lots of time or you want to add in an extra session you could do all the options. All the options are available in their journal. Alternatively you could encourage the young people to do further work on it at home during the week if they are interested and motivated.*

A: Gospel enquiry

Invite the group to listen carefully to the story and to think about the time, place and people involved. Perhaps you could ask a member of the group to read out loud.

> **Read the Gospel, Mark 12:28-31**
> "One of the scribes who had listened to them debating appreciated that Jesus had given a good answer and put a further question to him, 'Which is the first of all the commandments?' Jesus replied, 'This is the first: Listen, Israel, the Lord our God is the one, only Lord and you must love the Lord your God with all your heart, with all your soul, with all your mind and with all your strength. The second is this: You must love your neighbour as yourself. There is no commandment greater than these.'"
>
> **And discuss together…**
> - Who is in this story?
> - What happened?
> - What was said?
> - How do you think the people present would have reacted to this? Why?
> - What does this story tell us about what is important in our own lives?

Leader's ideas:
Repeat the story with a little background: Jesus was teaching in the Temple in Jerusalem. Lots of people had come to listen to Jesus and to ask him questions. Some of them were trying to catch Jesus out so that he would say something that would give them an excuse to have him arrested. This question asks what the greatest of the commandments is. It is referring to the ten commandments God gave to Moses. But Jesus doesn't just stick to what is in the ten commandments, he gives a new one: "Love your neighbour as yourself." This commandment is the basis for almost all of the ten commandments but rather than the language of "thou shalt not" which lots of the commandments use, it uses positive language, encouraging all God's people to love one another rather than think of narrow rules. It must have been a shocking thing for people to hear then.

From this Gospel reading we draw a lot of wisdom about how we, as Christians, should live our lives. Our lives should be lives based on love. A great saint, Augustine, once wrote:

> ### "Love God, and then do what you want."

Ask the young people what they think St Augustine meant. (Suggested answer: "He meant that if you place loving God first in your life, then all the things you will want to do will be good things because you will no longer want to do anything which causes harm.")

B: The beatitudes

Say to the group:
Jesus gave us principles to live our lives by in his teaching which we call the Beatitudes (or you could think of them as the "Be Attitudes" – ways of living). Let's read them together and think about them.

Read the Gospel, Matthew 5:3-12

> "How blessed are the poor in spirit: the kingdom of heaven is theirs.
> Blessed are the gentle: they shall have the earth as their inheritance.
> Blessed are those who mourn: they shall be comforted.
> Blessed are those who hunger and thirst for uprightness: they shall have their fill.
> Blessed are the merciful: they shall have mercy shown them.
> Blessed are the pure in heart: they shall see God.
> Blessed are the peacemakers: they shall be recognised as children of God.
> Blessed are those who are persecuted in the cause of uprightness: the kingdom of heaven is theirs.
> Blessed are you when people abuse you and persecute you and speak all kinds of calumny against you falsely on my account. Rejoice and be glad, for your reward will be great in heaven."

Ask the group : Do you think that this list of people actually offers a guide for how to be? What would a list of characteristics which we could draw from this reading look like? (You could write it down on a flip chart). (Suggested answer: be humble; be gentle; long for things to be better; be merciful; be pure in heart; be a peacemaker; stand up for what is right).

Ask the group whether they think these are good principles to live by today. Why?

GLOSSARY — The name "Beatitudes" comes from the Latin word *beatus* which means blessed or happy.

C: What does our faith say?

Say to the group: Jesus passed on his authority to his twelve apostles, before he ascended into heaven. Those twelve men continued to pass on their authority through ordaining others, whom we now call bishops. These bishops work together to continue to give us guidance as to how we should try to live. There are often things in our lives which Jesus never talked about, such as nuclear warfare, abortion, genetic engineering or the rights and wrongs of modern economic policies. For these things and a whole host of others, the Church provides teaching we can refer to in order to guide us.

Ask the group: Do you agree that we should listen to what the Church teaches?

Say to the group: We also believe that Jesus gave the Church seven sacraments, through which God continues to communicate to us and to offer us help. In the sacraments Jesus is present, showing us the love and support of God. God uses all our senses to communicate with us through the sacraments. We see, touch, hear, smell and even taste!

continued overleaf »

Ask the group: to list the sacraments (Baptism, Reconciliation, Holy Communion, Confirmation, Marriage, Sacrament of the Sick, Ordination). Then ask them to think about what senses are involved in each sacrament. Or you can just ask them to think about what senses are involved at confirmation and what this symbolises (e.g. the bishop lays his hands on you, using the sense of touch: this shows the moment when you receive the Holy Spirit).

ACE

This section is intended to show the Catholic faith working in some people's lives. Each week there will be a profile of a young person and of someone who has been motivated by their faith to do something amazing. These texts are also in the young people's journal. You could mention them as something for the young people to read during the week or you could make it the basis for a discussion in the whole group about living as a Christian.

Meet

Katherine

Hello, my name's Katherine, and I'm 15. My faith has a massive impact on my life.

When I go through tough personal experiences I always pray to God, and it helps me get through it, helps kind of relax me. It's like I'm having a personal conversation with a friend, someone I've known for ever.

My dad was in hospital about three years ago, and I found it quite hard to talk to anyone about it. So I turned to God and prayed to him, and I knew that other people were praying as well. And I felt that if other people were praying to God then it would be okay.

If I didn't have my faith, I'd be worried because I'd be thinking that nothing could improve. I think if I'm praying to someone, then life is going to get better.

Pelé

Ask any football fan to name some of the greatest footballers ever and one name is bound to come high up their list. Pelé. In his home nation, Brazil, he is nicknamed "O Rei do Futebol" – " the King of Football". He is the only footballer to have lifted the World Cup three times and has scored more goals for Brazil than any other player before or since. His heyday was the 1960s and 1970s but since his retirement from playing in 1977 he has used his fame and influence in both international football and to work for children living in poverty.

Pelé's real name is Edison Arantes do Nascimento. He was born to a poor family in a *favela* – a shanty town – in Sao Paolo in 1940. As a child he didn't own a football and played with a sock stuffed with newspaper. His dad, who had tried to be a professional footballer before injury ruined his career, taught Pelé how to play. Since he was talent spotted as a teenager Pelé has become one of the most famous footballers of all time and one of the greatest Catholic sportspeople the world has seen.

© Christopher Furlong/Getty Images 2007

QUOTE

"God gave me the gift of knowing how to play soccer – because it really is a gift from God – and my father taught me to use it, he taught me the importance of always being ready and prepared, and that in addition to being a good player I should also be a good man." Pelé

56

Deciding on your action

So far today we have thought about making decisions and about how we are called to love one another. We have also thought about how the Holy Spirit is always present to help and guide us. When we look at how our real lives and faith combine, it leads to action. Once we have thought through God's perspective on our lives we are ready to decide on an action.

Personal action:
Encourage the young people to commit to doing something during the next week which will help show love to another person. Ideally this should be as a result of their own notes about real life and faith. The action can be very small and hidden if they want. They can write the action down in their journal but they do not need to share it with the group at all.

To get their ideas started you could make some suggestions or ask some questions. Perhaps suggest doing something for someone in their family or being kind to someone at school. Or ask questions such as "Can you think of an elderly relative who might be glad to hear from you?"

Tell the young people that at each session they will be asked if they have done their action and whether they want to share their experience with the group. Remind them that they do not have to share or tell anyone about their action if they do not want to.

> **TIP** If your parish is supportive you could organise a helpful job for the young people to do within the parish – perhaps tidying up the benches after Mass, or handing out the hymn books before Mass, or taking up the offertory.

Say to the group:
Let's look back at the notes we made at the beginning. Think again about the decisions we have faced and what we were pleased with and what we were ashamed of. Remember that Jesus told us to love one another and gave us the gifts of the Holy Spirit to help us to achieve this.

How have you responded to the Beatitudes? Does this help you think how you can take action this week?

Group action:
Is there anything we can do as a group to take action on what you have been discussing today?

What can we pray about?

You can encourage the young people to see praying as one way of taking action as a group.

Ask everyone to write a very simple intention (e.g. "for victims of bullying", "for my little sister who is ill", etc.) on a small piece of paper. These will be used during the closing prayer. By now the group may know each other well enough to share their intentions aloud. You can ask the group if anyone feels ready, but be clear that there is no pressure and that they never need to share it with anyone but God unless they want to.

Before you begin the closing prayer section, encourage the young people to read through and fill in their journal during the week ahead. Remind them that it is a tool to help them on their journey to confirmation. Their journal contains lots more information and ideas than can be covered in each section.

TIP "If the young people are planning a service project for after confirmation, there maybe things they've noticed in today's discussion which they could help do something about."

QUOTE "The Christian does not think God will love us because we are good, but that God will make us good because God loves us." *C.S. Lewis*

PRAYER

You will need the candle and a basket or bowl for prayer intentions.

This short prayer and meditation can be done in church with candles lit and lights dimmed. Perhaps you could all gather in front of the sanctuary, sitting on the floor. If using the church isn't practical you could instead sit in a circle around the candle as at the beginning of the session. You can use all the prayer and meditation below or just the prayer if you prefer. You might find it helpful to have meditative music in the background and perhaps an image – whether a photo, a statue, an icon or a Bible – beside the candle and basket to act as a prayer focus.

Ask the young people to put their prayer intentions in the basket. They don't need to tell anyone what they have written. Invite the group to become still. Light the prayer candle again.

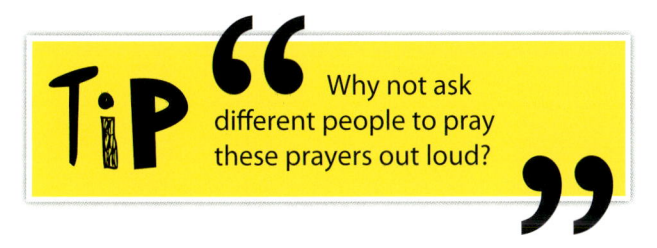

> **TIP** " Why not ask different people to pray these prayers out loud? "

> Lord, we gather here and bring our prayer intentions before you. We know that you will listen to our wants and needs and we know that you will respond with love towards us. Fill our hearts with your love and inspire us to be the best we can be by modelling ourselves on your example.
> Amen.

Silence for a short while

> *Read the following prayer which was written by St Thérèse of Lisieux, a French nun who died in 1897 aged just 24.*
>
> May today there be peace within.
> May you trust God that you are exactly where you are meant to be.
> May you not forget the infinite possibilities that are born of faith.
> May you use those gifts that you have received, and pass on the love that has been given to you.
> May you be content knowing you are a child of God.
> Let this presence settle into your bones, and allow your soul the freedom to sing, dance, praise and love.
> It is there for each and every one of us.
> Amen.

Final Prayer

Loving Lord Jesus,
As we go through life, we are constantly faced with decisions to make. We know that you have asked us to love one another. May that command influence all our decisions so that we may act with love and follow your ways.
Amen.

> **TIP** "If you would like a longer prayer session why not use some of the prayers and bible readings in the candidates' journals?"

As you end the session, remind the candidates of the date and time of the next session.

Session 5

Preparing for Reconciliation

Session 5
Preparing for Reconciliation

Aim:
To explore what the sacrament of reconciliation means to each young person and to the Church today and to plan a reconciliation service.

Leader's reflection:
How often do you go to confession? What do you feel about it? Do you find it helpful?

Have you ever seen a Catholic confession as part of a crime drama on TV? In films or TV shows? Wherever Catholic confession is shown it is an old fashioned image, often involving some great crime. This isn't the reality of the act of reconciliation today. The emphasis is not on "confessing" – reeling off a list of our many and various faults, but on "reconciling" – giving us the chance to renew our relationship with God and to make a fresh start.

In this session, you will plan a reconciliation service for your group of young people. Some of the group may be familiar with confession but others might not have been to confession since they made their first Holy Communion. By getting them involved in the preparation you are helping them to understand what the sacrament of reconciliation can mean to them.

> **TIP** "Maybe you could have a discussion with all the catechists about what reconciliation means for each one of you?"

You will need:
- Flip-chart paper and pens

Candidates will need:
- Their candidate journal and a pen

QUOTE "Be compassionate just as your Father is compassionate. Do not judge, and you will not be judged; do not condemn, and you will not be condemned; forgive, and you will be forgiven."
From the Gospel of St Luke

Notes and ideas for catechists:

There is a lot of flexibility about how you use this session and how you organise your service of reconciliation. The catechists and the Parish Priest will need to agree what is best for your parish. Here are a few ideas for you to discuss:

- Will you have the service of reconciliation on a separate day, or have it following directly on from this preparation session?

- This session is shorter than other sessions to allow you to have a service of reconciliation afterwards if you wish to. If you want to have the service on another date, then you could use the time left at the end of this session for something social. Think about what might work with your group. Perhaps showing a film, or having drinks and nibbles and a chance to chat, or even going on an outing to a bowling alley or something similar.

- Alternatively if it worked for your parish you could make this session and the service of reconciliation the focus for a whole-day-long session at a weekend. This could be treated as a day retreat for the group.

- Think about what resources you have in your parish. Will the Parish Priest, or another priest be available to hear individual confessions? How much input will he want to have into the planning of the service and how flexible is he willing to be about the format of the service? Will you have any parish musicians so you can choose hymns, or would it be appropriate to use recorded music or will the service be without music? Will you be able to print up service sheets for everyone?

- Think about the members of your group. Realistically, how much input do you think would work at this planning stage? What skills do they have? For a very motivated group they could prepare a drama based on one of the readings if your parish priest would like to include it before his homily. Or perhaps they could write their own prayers, or perform their own music. They might be able to come up with a creative approach to this service. If the group don't seem at all motivated, you might try to engage them by asking them simply to choose readings.

- The liturgy for a service of reconciliation can be flexible, but there are a few things which you really should have in your service. You will need an opening prayer, at least one scripture reading, an examination of conscience, a general confession of sins and individual confessions. But you could include more readings, hymns, prayers, a sermon, a sign of peace and a prayer or act of thanksgiving to finish. There is a suggested service in Appendix 1 to help you.

QUOTE "Confession heals, confession justifies, confession grants pardon of sin. All hope consists in confession. In confession there is a chance for mercy. Believe it firmly. Do not doubt, do not hesitate, never despair of the mercy of God. Hope and have confidence in confession." *St Isidore of Seville*

SEE

In this section we encourage the young people to examine the things that happen to them in their lives. Ask the group to look in their journals and complete the following questions:

When did you last have to admit to someone that you had done something wrong?
How did it make you feel?
What do you remember about the last time you went to confession to a priest?
How did it make you feel?

Then ask the group to get into small groups and write down on flip charts what words and images come into their minds when they think about going to confession. Encourage them to be honest.

Now ask the group to discuss forgiveness together:
What happens when people choose not to forgive people?
What happens when they do choose to forgive?
Ask the group to get into small groups and write their thoughts down on two sheets of flip-chart paper to feed back to the group.

QUOTE

"Without forgiveness there can be no future for a relationship between individuals or within and between nations." *Archbishop Emeritus Desmond Tutu of Cape Town*

JUDGE

A: Gospel enquiry

Do at least one of the sections below.

Invite the group to listen carefully to the story and to think about the time, place and people involved. Perhaps you could ask a member of the group to read. The Gospel text is printed in their journals.

Read the Gospel, Luke 5:17-25
"Now it happened that he was teaching one day… and now some men appeared bringing on a bed a paralysed man whom they were trying to bring in and lay down in front of him. But as they could find no way of getting the man through the crowd, they went up onto the top of the house and lowered him and his stretcher down through the tiles into the middle of the gathering, in front of Jesus. Seeing their faith he said, 'My friend, your sins are forgiven you.' The scribes and the Pharisees began to think this over. 'Who is this man, talking blasphemy? Who but God alone can forgive sins?' But Jesus, aware of their thoughts, made them this reply, 'What are these thoughts you have in your hearts? Which of these is easier: to say "Your sins are forgiven you" or to say "Get up and walk"? But to prove to you that the Son of man has authority on earth to forgive sins,' – he said to the paralysed man – 'I order you: get up and pick up your stretcher and go home.' And immediately before their very eyes he got up, picked up what he had been lying on and went home praising God."

And discuss together…
- Who is in this story?
- What happened?
- What was said?
- How do you think the man on the stretcher would have reacted to this? Why?
- How do you think the Pharisees and scribes would have reacted to this? Why?
- What does this story say about the forgiveness of sins?

Leader's ideas:
This story shows how things do not always happen as we think they will with Jesus. When we first heard this story about the man who is lowered from the roof, we probably expected Jesus to heal him because we have heard other stories about Jesus healing people. But the emphasis in this story is not on the man's physical healing. It is on Jesus' ability to forgive sins. This forgiveness has made the man whole in a more important way than healing his physical disability.

By showing that he can forgive sins and that he can also heal the physical disability, Jesus highlights the fact that he possesses God's power. The forgiveness of sins is invisible but the healing of the paralysed man is physical proof of that power. The scribes and Pharisees see Jesus as a threat, as he brings a powerful and popular new form of the religion they perceive themselves as controlling. Even this display of power doesn't convince them that Jesus is the Messiah, and the Jewish authorities will continue to try to bring Jesus down.

QUOTE "To those who have been far away from the sacrament of reconciliation and forgiving love, I make this appeal: Come back to this source of grace; do not be afraid! Christ himself is waiting for you. He will heal you, and you will be at peace with God!" *Pope John Paul II*

B: What does our faith say?

Today we have the chance to plan our celebration of the sacrament of reconciliation. We want to emphasise CELEBRATE! This is not a chore. It is not something to be nervous of. It is a wonderful gift that the Church gives us. In the last few weeks we have all shared what is important to us and how we think we should live our lives and how God calls us to live.

However, we know that we all fail sometimes. When we fail we need to find a way to make peace, to reconcile ourselves, with God. Think about when you have an argument with your parents. You don't stop loving them and they don't stop loving you. But you can't ignore a big upset. Even though you don't stop loving each other, you still have to make up. It might just be a smile. It might be saying sorry. It may be a hug or a handshake. We need to find a way to express our sorrow and forgiveness and to show that everything is ok.

It is exactly the same with God. Just as we find a way to communicate forgiveness, he finds a way too: in the sacrament of reconciliation. Sometimes you need to give someone a hug to express forgiveness, and that is what God does for us in this sacrament. It's God's language. As we hear God communicating to us, through the words of the priest, it is a chance for us not only to say sorry but for us to really KNOW that God has forgiven us. It doesn't mean he ever stopped loving us. But sometimes we need to know it, and the sacrament of reconciliation gives us that opportunity: it is like a hug from God – a concrete sign of God's love and forgiveness for us.

Ask the group to discuss what they think about this, considering the sacrament to be a sign of God's love. What other images from their own lives could they suggest reconciliation is like? (This might help them plan some creative aspects of the liturgy in the "Act" section)

C: A sacramental sign – the priest

The sacrament of reconciliation is also our chance to say sorry to the whole community. We are all members of a community – of the parish, the school, the nation, the whole Church. Whenever I do something wrong I hurt the community but I can't say sorry to them all. But I can say sorry to the priest who acts on behalf of the whole community. I am not just saying sorry to God, but I am also saying sorry to everyone else and hearing that I am forgiven too.

If your priest is present invite the young people to ask questions, which might help them prepare for celebrating the sacrament.

QUOTE

"Before you speak, it is necessary for you to listen, for God speaks in the silence of the heart."
Mother Teresa

ACE

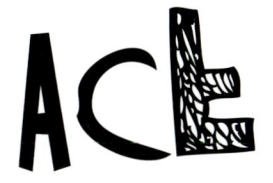

Group action: preparing the service
There is a question and answer section in their journals at this point which aims to give some answers to questions young people frequently have about going to confession. You can direct them towards this as something for them to read before the reconciliation service takes place.

So far we have thought about what the sacrament of reconciliation is and how we have experienced it. Now we are going to prepare our own service of reconciliation.

Give the group tasks to do to prepare the service. This could be as simple as choosing readings from a selection given in their journals, or getting them to plan a drama or make a piece of artwork.

To help, you can use the texts for a service of reconciliation in Appendix 1 of this book. This is just a basic service with a few options and ideas added in. You can use as much of it as you like.

QUOTE

"There is more joy in heaven over a converted sinner than over a righteous person standing firm…. A farmer has greater love for land which bears fruitfully, after he has cleared it of thorns, than for land which never had thorns but which never yielded a fruitful harvest." *St Gregory the Great*

Personal action:
Ask the young people whether they did the action they decided on at last week's session. Remind them that it isn't too late if they haven't. They can always do it this week alongside their next action.

Ask the young people how they found doing their action.

Tell the group:
Today we have looked at what the sacrament of reconciliation can mean in our lives. Before we receive the sacrament of reconciliation in our service, we can prepare our hearts in this time we have before the service.

Encourage the young people to think about their failings and weaknesses and to offer them to God in their hearts. They might want to write some things down to help them prepare for making their confession.

To get their ideas started you could make some suggestions or ask some questions. Perhaps suggest thinking about whether there are people they have been unkind to, or argued with, or things they have purposely avoided doing which would have helped someone.

TIP

" In the candidates' journals there is guidance about what to do and say in confession. You could ask the group to read this before their service of reconciliation. "

PRAYER

Do not do this section if you are going to hold your service of reconciliation immediately after this session is finished!

Dear Lord, today we have been preparing to meet you in the sacrament of reconciliation. May we spend this time of prayer remembering our failings but also being confident that we will soon be fully reconciled to you through your gift of confession. Amen.

Silence for a short while.

Read the following prayer which was written by St Francis of Assisi in the 13th century.

Lord, make me an instrument of your peace.
Where there is hatred, let me sow love;
where there is injury, pardon;
where there is doubt, faith;
where there is despair, hope;
where there is darkness, light;
and where there is sadness, joy.

O Divine Master, grant that I may not so much seek
to be consoled as to console;
to be understood as to understand;
to be loved as to love.
For it is in giving that we receive;
it is in pardoning that we are pardoned;
and it is in dying that we are born to eternal life. Amen.

Final Prayer

Loving Father,
You lift us up from our failings and show us perfection.
You do not offer us what we deserve. Instead you offer us amazing gifts.
You have given us your Son, and eternal life.
May we return to you through our service of reconciliation
with hearts full of thankfulness and hope.
Amen.

As you end the session, remind the candidates of the date and time of the service of reconciliation if it is to be held at a later date.

Session 6

Time Out – Prayer and the Mass

Session 6
Time Out – Prayer and the Mass

Aim:
To explore our understanding of the Mass and our participation within it.

Leader's reflection:
Can you remember your First Holy Communion? What do you remember about that day? How do you feel when you go to Mass these days? Does it still feel special? Sometimes, when we do something regularly it becomes a habit and we hardly think about what we are doing. The challenge is to recognise that it is special every time we go, no matter how we are feeling at the time. In today's session you can help the group to remember how special their First Holy Communion day was and encourage them to see every time they go to Mass as an opportunity to take time with God and to be aware of the special gift we are given in the Eucharist.

> **TIP** Maybe you could have a discussion with all the catechists about what the Mass means for each one of you?

You will need:
- A candle and something to light it with
- Some relaxing/meditative music
- Flip-chart paper and pens
- Small pieces of paper for the young people to write their prayer intentions on and some pens/pencils to write with (you might want double the usual amount of pieces of paper if you choose to add in a thanksgiving prayer this session)
- A basket or bowl to place the prayer intentions in at the end of the session (you might want two for this session)

Candidates will need:
- Their candidate journal and a pen

QUOTE **"Take it and eat… this is my body."**
From the Gospel of St Matthew

Begin with a prayer…

As the young people begin to arrive have the lights in the room dimmed, a candle lit in the centre. As each person arrives, invite them to sit quietly in a circle around the candle. Perhaps play some reflective music in the background.

> Lord Jesus,
> We are gathered together here again to prepare for the sacrament of confirmation. We ask that you will guide us and inspire us as we have fun, listen, learn and take part in this session today. Thank you for your presence here with us today and always.
> Amen.

TIP: "This prayer is also printed in the candidates' books. Perhaps ask a volunteer to pray it out loud while everyone adopts a posture of their choice, conducive to prayer."

To get us started…

To get everyone started, begin with a group exercise to help everyone feel comfortable in each other's company. Use the following activity, or another one of your choice.

Come to order
The aim of this game is to get the group communicating with each other and in the process to help them get to know each other a little more. The game simply involves lining up in order of a chosen rule (height, hair length, age, etc.).

If you have a very large group you might want to split them up into groups of 10 for this activity, with a catechist or a candidate as group leader, giving out the rules.

Get everyone to stand up. Then ask them to form a line at the front in order of height, smallest to tallest. Each person has to negotiate with the others to find the correct place in the line for them.

Then change the criterion and form a new line. Criteria you could use include: length of hair, age, number of hours they slept last night, shoe size or alphabetically by first name to name but a few.

The moral of this game is that we are all different and putting us in ranks only shows one aspect of ourselves. Rather than viewing ourselves in comparison to others we can all remember how God views us: as equally special individuals, created in God's image and worthy of love.

TIP: "Try and rig the criteria so that no one ends up at one end of the line all the time!"

SEE

In this section we encourage the young people to examine the things that happen to them in their lives.

Ask the group to think on their own and write the answer to the following question in their journal:

What do you remember about your First Holy Communion?

Ask the group to get into pairs or small groups. What has stuck in their minds from their First Holy Communion?

You can help the group to discuss their answers and challenge the group to be honest about their answers. It doesn't matter what they remember. The answers will be varied from the clothes, or the parties, or the presents or money they received.

Ask them to feed back to the whole group (you can write answers on a flip chart if you like) and then ask them to get back into pairs or small groups and think about the following question:

> **Looking back on it now, do you think that these were the most important things that happened that day? If not, what do you think the most important things were?**

Ask the young people to feed back their responses to the whole group.

Remind the group: **The Church tells us that the most important thing about our First Holy Communion day was receiving Jesus in Holy Communion.**

Then ask:

> **How do you take time out from the busy-ness of school and daily life?**
> **Have you ever experienced or thought of prayer and going to Church as taking time out?**
> **What do you think might stop some young people from thinking of this as valuable time out?**

Note to leader
At this stage, no one is judging what the young people are saying. As group leader you do not need to "correct" anything which goes against Church teaching here. The "Judge" section of this session will provide an opportunity to reflect more deeply in faith. You can encourage the group to explore not just whether they believe in God, but what they believe about God (e.g. God is loving, God is good, or God doesn't care about us, I feel angry with God for making the world this way, etc.).

QUOTE

"What wonderful majesty! What stupendous condescension! O sublime humility! That the Lord of the whole universe, God and the Son of God, should humble Himself like this under the form of a little bread, for our salvation." *St Francis of Assisi*

JUDGE

*Do at least **two** of the three sections below. All the options are available in the young people's journals so if you don't do all the sections you could encourage the young people to do further work on it at home during the week if they are interested and motivated.*

A: Gospel enquiry

Invite the group to listen carefully to the story and to think about the time, place and people involved. Perhaps you could ask a member of the group to read. The Gospel text is printed in their journals.

Read the Gospel, Luke 9:11-17
"Jesus made the crowds welcome and talked to them about the kingdom of God; and he cured those who were in need of healing. It was late afternoon when the Twelve came up to him and said, 'Send the people away and they can go to the villages and farms round about to find lodging and food; for we are in a lonely place here.' He replied, 'Give them something to eat yourselves.' But they said, 'We have no more than five loaves and two fish, unless we are to go ourselves and buy food for all these people.' For there were about five thousand men. But he said to his disciples, 'Get them to sit down in parties of about fifty.' They did so and made them all sit down. Then he took the five loaves and the two fish, raised his eyes to heaven, and said the blessing over them; then he broke them and handed them to his disciples to distribute among the crowd. They all ate as much as they wanted, and when the scraps left over were collected they filled twelve baskets."

And discuss together…
- Who is in this story?
- What happened?
- What was said?
- How do you think the disciples would have reacted to this? Why?
- How do you think the people who had come to listen to Jesus would have reacted to this? Why?
- Does this story tell us anything about going to Mass?

Leader's ideas:
This reading from St Luke's Gospel comes from a section where Jesus gives lots of public teaching, works lots of miracles and travels around gathering more and more followers. It must have been an exciting time to be around Jesus.

His popularity creates a problem for Jesus' twelve apostles. What do they do with such large crowds? Jesus has the answer. He works a miracle to provide more than enough food for everyone. He shows the crowds that Jesus doesn't just give you enough of what you need in life, he gives you even more than you need.

It is the same when we go to Mass. When we go to Mass we remember the great outpouring of love which Jesus made on the cross for us. Jesus brings us back to God by showing us that our faults and failings are forgiven. But Jesus didn't just die on the cross for us, he rose from the dead, showing us the eternal life which is promised for us too. He gave us a way to remember his death and resurrection, and he gave us a way to share in his risen life, by sharing his body and blood in Mass.

B: What does our faith say?

Say to the group: The Church tells us to go to Mass every Sunday. Why? Well, we could look at it as a set of rules and regulations as children might think about what their parents say; or we could have the more mature approach like when we realise that actually our parents ask us to do things because they love us and want the best for us. It's the same with the Church. Mass is good for us, and the Church encourages us to go because it knows this.

Going to Mass is like going away from our homes, studies and everyday life, just like the people in the Gospel who went away to listen to Jesus. In fact, going to Mass can be like going away on a holiday – a 45-minute holiday! When we go away we tend to say that we're leaving everything at home and not taking our worries with us – the course work and revision can wait until I get back! We pack a case and head off to relax for a week or two. Well, that's not entirely true. Usually we do, almost without knowing it, take the time away to sort a few things out, to work out some of the big issues in life. Yes, we stop worrying about the small insignificant stuff but sometimes, with the larger situations in life, we find that we come back from time away with a new perspective on them and with new enthusiasm to address them. It's the same with going to Mass. Each week we take time away from our everyday life, but bring all the joys and concerns of life with us. We offer all of these things to God in the Mass, so that God can begin to sort them out. Jesus feeds us with his words, and with his presence in the Eucharist, so that we can go back to the world refreshed and with new energy to live life as God wants.

Do you agree that going to Mass should be like this?
Can we consider that taking time to pray might be like this too?

C: A sacramental sign

At each Mass we offer bread and wine, usually with an offertory procession. Two members of the congregation, on our behalf, take the simple elements of bread and wine and give them to the priest, who for us at that moment stands in the place of Christ. What's happening there? We are offering all the real stuff of our lives, the work of our hands and the fruit of the earth. Through that bread and wine we offer all we've achieved, all our joys alongside all our concerns and worries. The priest, representing Christ, then takes our real lives and offers them to the Father in heaven. Then something amazing happens to the bread and wine, for the Church tells us that when we receive Holy Communion we are receiving the real presence of Jesus. It's no longer bread and wine, but the life-giving presence of God. Everything we have offered in the bread and the wine has been made perfect – more than perfect – and been transformed for us into the best gift we have in the entire universe. All of our joys, all of our worries and all of our sorrows are made into something amazing. And we are offered this amazing gift beyond all our imaginings to feed us and nourish us for the return to our daily lives, so that we can transform our lives and the world around us.

The offertory, then, is a part of the Mass when we should be praying most! We should be letting God know what we are offering through the bread and wine, what bits of our real lives. What would you offer this week?

There is space in their journals if they want to write their thoughts down.

QUOTE **"Then he took a cup, and when he had given thanks he handed it to them, and all drank from it, and he said to them, 'This is my blood, the blood of the covenant, poured out for many.'"** *From the Gospel of St Mark*

ACE

This section is intended to show the Catholic faith working in some people's lives. Each week there will be a profile of a young person and of someone who has been motivated by their faith to do something amazing. These texts are also in the young people's journal. You could mention them as something for the young people to read during the week or you could make it the basis for a discussion in the whole group to enable each individual and the whole group to decide how they are going to take action. If you decide to make this a topic for discussion, here are a few questions to get you started.

How do you think Conor might have felt if he didn't go to Mass?

How do you think going to Mass helps the Mizen family come to terms with the loss of their son Jimmy? Why?

Meet

Conor

I'm from the north-east of England, and I'm a Catholic because I believe the earth has more relevance than just us being here. I think there's something bigger out there. I go to church even though lots of people tell me it's a waste of time. I do that because I believe in God, and it's a tiny thing that God asks us, to go to church for one hour every week, after all he does for us, just so we can celebrate him, talk about him and be educated about him. If people just called me all the time asking for things, but never did anything in return, that would agitate me.

Going to church furthers my knowledge about Christianity and about Jesus and how he lived his life. It educates me about what I believe in, rather than just "being Catholic" and not knowing anything about it. Sometimes, of course, I don't feel like going to Mass, but even if I go and just sit there I know that God is still present with me.

Jimmy Mizen's family

The day after his sixteenth birthday, Jimmy Mizen and his brother popped into a bakery on their way to buy Jimmy's first ever lottery ticket. In the bakery they were taunted by a nineteen-year-old who then attacked and murdered Jimmy with a broken glass serving dish after he refused to go outside to have a fight.

Jimmy's whole family grieved the loss of this gentle, peaceful young man. His six brothers and two sisters, together with his parents, Barry and Margaret Mizen, decided that some good needed to come out of Jimmy's death. At his funeral his dad said: "Perhaps we all need to look to ourselves and look to the values we would like and our responses to situations in our life. Sometimes we might be drawn into certain ways of living. It is our choice but change has got to come from all of us."

Jimmy's mother wrote about how the family's Catholic faith helped her, in an open letter she wrote to Jimmy after his death: "My faith keeps me going. You know how much I like going to church and I couldn't miss Mass, it gets me through the week. I miss seeing you at the back, at 6ft 4in head and shoulders above everyone else. When tears come at night me and dad say a prayer together. Lighting candles in church also helps me feel better." The family decided not to let hatred take over their lives. Now a foundation in Jimmy's name runs a coffee shop and organises local apprenticeships, it funds minibuses for community projects and perhaps most importantly it campaigns against violence, promoting a legacy of peace.

QUOTE

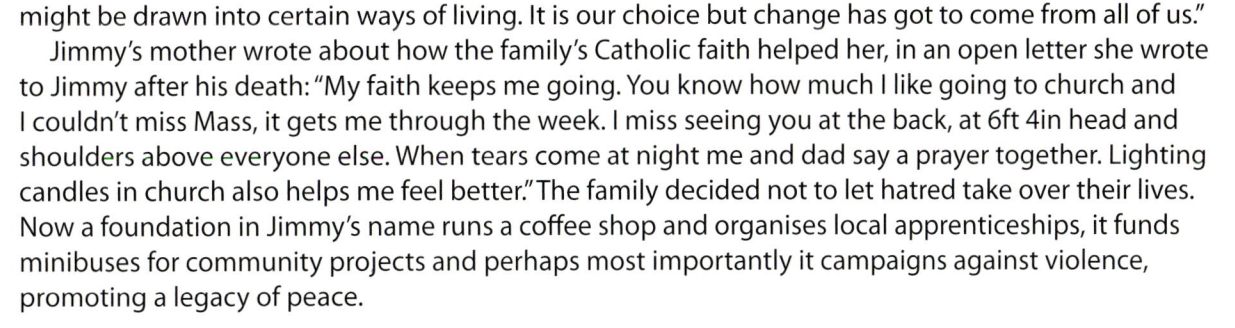

"Sometimes when I think about what's happened to Jimmy I just want to crawl into a hole, but I pray, I pray to the Holy Spirit, and I am comforted and uplifted and somehow receive the strength to cope." *Margaret Mizen*

Deciding on your action

So far we have looked at how going to Mass and receiving Communion allow us to share Christ in a special way. We have also thought about how prayer and the Mass give us an opportunity to take time out with God, as well as some of the challenges to it.

When we look at how our real lives and faith combine, it leads to action. Once we have thought through God's perspective on our lives we are ready to decide on an action.

Personal action:
Ask the young people whether they did do the action they decided on at last week's session. Remind them that it isn't too late if they haven't. They can always do it this week alongside their next action.

Ask the young people how they found doing their action.

Tell the group:
Today we have looked at what we remembered about our First Holy Communion days. We have also thought about what is important about receiving Communion and about why we go to Mass.

Is there anything you can do in these areas of difficulty to try and live as Christians?

*Encourage the young people to commit to doing something during the next week in which they will act as a Christian in a way that they find difficult. Ideally this should be as a result of their own notes about **real life** and **faith**. The action can be very small and hidden if they want. They can write the action down in their journal but they do not need to share it with the group at all.*

To get their ideas started you could make some suggestions or ask some questions. Perhaps suggest trying to include someone they would normally try to avoid at school. Or not doing something they know is wrong even though other people are doing it. Or ask questions such as "Can you think of a time this week when you can show someone that you recognise that they are valued?"

Tell the young people that at each session they will be asked if they have done their action and whether they want to share their experience with the group. Remind them that they do not have to share or tell anyone about their action if they do not want to.

Group action:
Ask the group to think about the following questions:

Is there anything we can do as a group to take action on what you have been discussing today?
What can we pray about?

You can encourage the young people to see praying as one way of taking action as a group.

Perhaps this session you could encourage everyone to write down something they would like to thank God for – this could be instead of, or in addition to, writing down a prayer intention. These will be used during the closing prayer.

> **TIP** " If the young people are planning a service project, there may be things they've noticed in today's discussion which they could help do something about.

Before you begin the closing prayer section, encourage the young people to read through and fill in their journal during the week ahead. Remind them that it is a tool to help them on their journey to confirmation. Their journal contains lots more information and ideas than can be covered in each section.

QUOTE **"If angels could be jealous of men, they would be so for one reason: Holy Communion."** *St Maximilian Kolbe*

PRAYER

You will need the candle and a basket or bowl for the prayer intentions.

This short prayer and meditation can be done in church with candles lit and lights dimmed. Perhaps you could all gather in church, sitting on the floor close to the altar. If using the church isn't practical you could instead sit in a circle around the candle as at the beginning of the session. You can use all the prayer and meditation below or just the prayer if you prefer. You might find it helpful to have meditative music in the background and perhaps an image – whether a photo, a statue, an icon or a Bible – beside the candle and basket to act as a prayer focus.

Ask the young people to put their prayer intentions in the basket. If you like, you could have two baskets, one for the thanksgiving prayers and one for their prayer intentions. They don't need to tell anyone what they have written. Invite the group to become still. Light the prayer candle again.

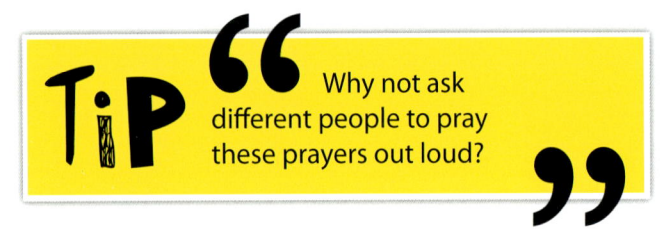

> **TIP** "Why not ask different people to pray these prayers out loud?"

Lord Jesus Christ,
In our lives you have given us everything we need and very much more. You came to earth and died on a cross, in forgiveness of sins. You rose again, showing us the way to eternal salvation. And we can experience your presence within us through the gift of Holy Communion which you have given us. Thank you for giving us the gift of yourself in Holy Communion and for giving me the chance to share in it.
Amen.

Silence for a short while

Read the following excerpt from the first letter St Paul wrote to the Christian community in the city of Corinth (1 Corinthians 10:16-17)
"The blessing cup which we bless, is it not a sharing in the blood of Christ; and the loaf of bread which we break, is it not a sharing in the body of Christ? And as there is one loaf, so we, although there are many of us, are one single body, for we all share in the one loaf."

Final Prayer

Thank you, Lord Jesus, for guiding me in my life so far. Please be a companion to me throughout my life. Help me to remember that whatever the future holds for me, you will always be present. With you I know that nothing will happen which I cannot cope with when I have the gifts of your help and strength. Amen.

As you end the session, remind the candidates of the date and time of the next session.

SESSION 7

FAITH... IN WHAT?
WHAT DO YOU BELIEVE?

Session 7
FAITH... IN WHAT? WHAT DO YOU BELIEVE?

Aim:
To explore our answers to the questions "What do I believe?" and "What do we believe?"

Leader's reflection:
Do you ever take time to think about what is really important in your life or are you always too busy rushing around, trying to get things done? Take a moment now to think about what your priorities are at the moment and what you think you would like them to be. Are they the same? Or do you need to make some changes to get life back in order? We all find ourselves caught up in the whirlwind of everyday busy-ness. It is easy to lose sight of what is important. In today's session you will help the group to explore what is really important to each one of them. It's a useful exercise for everyone throughout life!

> **TIP** If there is a team of catechists in your parish, perhaps you could meet together for a few minutes before every session and read and think through the leader's reflection each week?

You will need:
- Post-It notes (or similar), at least enough for one for each young person. They need to be the right size to fit on your forehead!
- A candle and something to light it with
- Some relaxing/meditative music
- Flip-chart paper and pens
- Small pieces of paper for the young people to write their prayer intentions on and some pens/pencils to write with
- A basket or something to place the prayer intentions in at the end of the session

Candidates will need:
- Their candidate journal and a pen

QUOTE "Everyone who believes may have eternal life."
From the Gospel of St John

Begin with a prayer…

As the young people begin to arrive have the lights in the room dimmed, a candle lit in the centre. As each person arrives, invite them to sit quietly in a circle around the candle. Perhaps play some reflective music in the background.

> Lord Jesus,
> As we gather here today we ask that you will bless our time together. As we explore our beliefs and the things we hold most important in our lives, we ask that you will guide us and give us wisdom and insight so that we can learn how to be fully the people you have created us to be.
> Amen.

TIP " This prayer is also printed in the candidates' books. Perhaps ask a volunteer to pray it out loud while everyone adopts a posture of their choice, conducive to prayer. "

To get us started…

To get everyone started, begin with a group exercise to help everyone feel comfortable in each other's company. Use the following activity, or another one of your choice.

Who am I?

The aim of the game is for each person to guess what name is written on the Post-It on their forehead by asking their team-mates questions.

Get into groups of about five or six people.

You can either prepare Post-Its in advance with the names of famous people on, or you can make part of the activity getting the young people to think of and write the name of a famous person on a Post-It and stick it on a team-mate's forehead without them seeing.

Each young person will have a Post-It note with the name of a famous person stuck on their forehead. They must not know in advance what that name is. They then ask their team-mates questions to find out who they are. The questions need to be in the form of "I" questions: e.g. "Am I alive or dead?"; "Am I a movie star?"; "Am I a footballer?"; etc. Answers can only be "Yes" or "No".

When everyone has found out "who they are", call the whole group back together.

By playing this game we have been trying to work out what is recognisable about people – what they look like, what they do, what they have achieved. But one thing which is hard for someone else to ever know is what a person truly believes. Yet this is probably the most important thing in anyone's life. Now we will explore what each of us really believe to be important.

SEE

In this section we encourage the young people to examine the things that happen to them in their lives.

What do you believe to be the most important thing in life?

Ask the young people the question above and get them into small groups to discuss it. They can come up with any answer (some suggested ideas to discuss: money, love, family, friends, music, sport, etc.). Group members don't need to agree with one another. Ask one member of the group to write down all the answers to share with everyone.

> **TIP:** It often helps to allow the young people to discuss their responses in pairs before sharing them with the group.

Why?

Now ask the young people (still in the small groups) to think about why they believe that. What experiences in their lives have caused them to believe that? Ask them for specific examples. Don't gloss over it if there are disagreements within the group. Allow everyone to share their experiences, positive or negative. Spend time allowing discussion so that everyone can examine how experiences shape our beliefs.

Bring the groups together and share what you have learned. You might want to take some more time for discussion as you do this.

Next get everyone back into their small groups and ask the following question:

What do you believe about God?

You may have already discussed God as part of the first question above, but ensure everyone has the chance to say what they believe about God. At this stage all answers are valid, so as group leader you do not need to "correct" anything which goes against Church teaching here. The "Judge" section of this session will provide Catholic teaching on belief. You can encourage the group to explore not just whether they believe in God, but what they believe about God (e.g. God is loving, God is good, or God doesn't care about us, I feel angry with God for making the world this way, etc.).

Bring the groups together again and share what you have learned. Make time for discussion here if it is needed.

Say to the group:

This is our last session of learning on this journey towards confirmation. Next session we will be preparing and rehearsing for the Confirmation Mass. So today we look at a very important part of the Mass. At every Sunday Mass we say the Creed together (declaring that "I believe in One God…"). At our Confirmation Mass, before we actually get confirmed, we will stand together before the bishop and the whole parish and declare what we believe, when we renew our baptismal promises.

> **TIP:** The words of the Creed are printed in the candidates' journals. Perhaps you could encourage them to read it before the next session.

JUDGE

*Do at least **two** of the three sections below. All the options are available in the young people's journals so if you don't do all the sections you could encourage the young people to do further work on it at home during the week if they are interested and motivated.*

A: Gospel Enquiry

Invite the group to listen carefully to the story and to think about the time, place and people involved. Perhaps you could ask a member of the group to read. The Gospel text is printed in their journals.

Read the Gospel, Matthew 16:13-17

"When Jesus came to the region of Caesarea Philippi he put this question to his disciples, 'Who do people say the Son of man is?' And they said, 'Some say John the Baptist, some Elijah, and others Jeremiah or one of the prophets.' 'But you,' he said, 'who do you say I am?' Then Simon Peter spoke up and said, 'You are the Christ, the Son of the living God.' Jesus replied, 'Simon, son of Jonah, you are a blessed man! Because it was no human agency that revealed this to you but my Father in heaven. So I now say to you: you are Peter and on this rock I will build my community. And the gates of the underworld can never overpower it.'"

And discuss together…

- Who is in this story?
- What happened?
- What was said?
- How do you think the apostles felt about being asked this question?
- Why do you think Jesus chose Peter to lead the Church?
- What does this story say about what we believe about Jesus?

Leader's ideas:

Jesus knows he is going to Jerusalem to die and he is making plans for the future of his followers. He chooses Simon, because Simon has recognised Jesus for who Jesus truly is. Jesus gives him a new name, Peter, which means "rock". Because Peter truly believes in Jesus, Peter will become the leader of the apostles and the whole Church. After Jesus died, rose again and went up to heaven, Peter led the Church, helping it to spread and grow around the world. He became the first pope and was put to death for his beliefs in Rome.

In the Gospel reading we heard that many people in Jesus' time did not know who Jesus was, so when they were asked who he was they guessed. They chose important prophets like John the Baptist. Simon Peter knew what he believed and wasn't afraid to say it. He told Jesus that he believed Jesus was the Christ (the chosen one) and the Son of God.

Tell the group:

At your confirmation you will be asked to state your beliefs. Even though many people in our world do not recognise who God is, you will say in front of your friends and families, and in front of God, that you believe in God.

Get into small groups and ask them to discuss the following questions and feed back to the whole group.

- What difficulties do you think people face in standing up for what they believe in?
- Are you prepared to speak about your faith when you are asked?

B: What does our faith say?

During your confirmation the bishop will ask you to renew your baptismal promises. These promises were made on your behalf by your parents and godparents when you were baptised. At your confirmation they are your way of saying, "Yes, I believe".

You will say that you believe:
- That good is better than evil
- That God is three persons, the Father, the Son and the Holy Spirit
- That you believe in the catholic Church and its teachings

Ask the young people to look at some of the text from the rite of renewal of baptismal promises which are printed in their journals (they are also printed below). Give them some time to read them alone and then ask them to discuss their answers to the following questions. They may want to make notes in their journal.

- Do you believe in the power of evil?
- How do you imagine God the Father?
- Who is Jesus for you?
- Have you ever been aware of the Holy Spirit (God's presence) acting in your life?
- When you say "I believe in the catholic Church" what images do you think of? A building? People? The Pope?

The bishop questions the candidates:

Do you reject Satan and all his works and all his empty promises?
CANDIDATES: I do.

Do you believe in God, the Father Almighty, Creator of heaven and earth?
CANDIDATES: I do.

Do you believe in Jesus Christ, his only Son, our Lord, who was born of the Virgin Mary, was crucified, died and was buried, rose from the dead and is now seated at the right hand of the Father?
CANDIDATES: I do.

Do you believe in the Holy Spirit, the Lord, the giver of life, who came upon the apostles at Pentecost and today is given to you sacramentally in confirmation?
CANDIDATES: I do.

Do you believe in the holy catholic Church, the communion of saints, the forgiveness of sins, the resurrection of the body and life everlasting?
CANDIDATES: I do.

QUOTE "I could not say I believe. I know! I have had the experience of being gripped by something that is stronger than myself, something that people call God." *Carl Jung, one of the founders of modern psychology*

C: A sacramental sign

Say to the group:
When we go to Mass, we believe that Christ is present:
He is present in the word of God proclaimed in the readings and the Gospel at the Mass.
He is present in the Eucharist, Holy Communion, celebrated on the altar.
He is present in the priest who stands in the place of Christ for us when he celebrates the Mass.

We also believe that Christ is present in the people gathered together. As a people, united together in church, joined in our belief, we are a visible sign of being many parts of one body. We remain a sign of Christ to the world as we leave church and return to our daily lives, still united in our belief and commitment to others.

- Can you think of other times and situations where many people are united together in common belief?
- How important is it for us to feel that we share common beliefs with others?
- How can the believing community of the Church be a sign of Christ to others? Can you, as a group, be a sign of Christ to others? If you have any ideas take them into the ACT section.

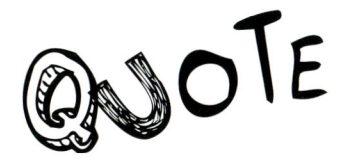

QUOTE

"It is by believing with the heart that you are justified, and by making the declaration with your lips that you are saved."

From the letter St Paul wrote to the Romans

ACE

This section is intended to show the Catholic faith working in some people's lives. Each week there is a profile of a young person and of someone who has been motivated by their faith to do something amazing. These texts are also in the young people's journal. You could mention them as something for the young people to read during the week or you could make it the basis for a discussion in the whole group to enable each individual and the whole group to decide how they are going to take action. If you decide to make this a topic for discussion, here are a few questions to get you started.

How do your beliefs make you live your life differently from people you know who do not believe in the same things? What do you admire about Maximilian Kolbe? Do you think he did the right thing when he offered himself in Auschwitz?

Meet

Nicolette

My faith gives me something to rely on. I like the fact that I can pray to God and communicate with God. I ask for things, I thank him for living every day of my life. I'm able to pray to God whenever I'm in need, for example when I'm in an exam, I pray to God, when some of my family members are in need I pray to God: it brings a connection that I need, something greater. I feel that humans need something greater, for them to experience life, to live a good life. Without something greater there is nothing to aspire to be.

In order to live a good life in my opinion you have to fulfill your potential. Fulfilling your potential is doing your calling, whatever you have to do, whatever job or career, do well in school, and be able to work and help others.

QUOTE

"Then they said to him 'What must we do if we are to carry out God's work?' Jesus gave them this answer: 'This is carrying out God's work; you must believe in the one he has sent.'" *From the Gospel of St John*

Meet

Maximilian Kolbe

St Maximilian Kolbe died as Prisoner 16670 in Auschwitz concentration camp on 14 August 1941.

Fr Maximilian Kolbe was a Franciscan friar and a priest. Long before his extraordinary death he had already achieved great things. He set up a huge religious community in Poland, then went on missions to establish churches in Japan and India. He later returned to Poland and ran the publishing company and radio station dedicated to Mary, the Mother of God, which he had established.

© Catholic News Service

During the 1930s he openly spoke out against the Nazis, and when they invaded Poland, Kolbe was imprisoned twice. The first time he was released after three months, but he didn't stop speaking out. His second imprisonment took him to the concentration camp in Auschwitz. Again he stayed a prisoner for three months, but this time his release came from death.

One day a prisoner escaped from Auschwitz. The camp commander demanded that ten prisoners be put to death to be an example to prevent others from escaping. Ten were chosen at random, but Fr Maximilian stepped forward and offered to take the place of one man who he knew was a husband and father. Francis Gajowniczek was allowed to live and Fr Maximilian was sent to die in his place. Fr Maximilian died of an injection of poison after four days in darkness with no food or water.

When Pope John Paul made him a saint in 1982, there was a special guest in the congregation – Francis Gajowniczek.

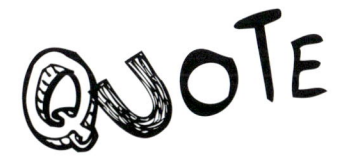

QUOTE

"Beyond armies of occupation and the hecatombs of extermination camps, there are two irreconcilable enemies in the depth of every soul: good and evil, sin and love. And what use are the victories on the battlefield if we are ourselves defeated in our innermost personal selves?" *St Maximilian Kolbe*

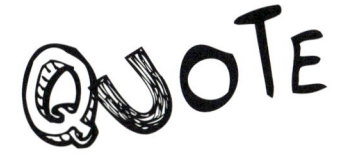

QUOTE

"Maximilian did not die but 'gave his life ... for his brother.' In that death, terrible from the human point of view, there was the whole definitive greatness of the human act and of the human choice. He spontaneously offered himself up to death out of love." *Pope John Paul II*

Deciding on your action

So far we have looked at what we believe and what that means in our lives. We have also looked at the promises we will make at our confirmation.

When we look at how our real lives and faith combine, it leads to action. Once we have thought through God's perspective on our lives we are ready to decide on an action.

Personal action:
Ask the young people whether they did do the action they decided on at last week's session. Remind them that it isn't too late if they haven't. They can always do it this week alongside their next action.

Ask the young people how they found doing their action.

Tell the group:
We believe in God, who lives in a community of three persons. The Father, Son and Holy Spirit live together in love. This model of the Trinity is the best example we have of how we should always try to live with one another in loving ways.

The model of the Trinity living together is our inspiration for action this week.

To get their ideas started you could make some suggestions or ask some questions.
- *What action can you take?*
- *Is there someone in your life, maybe a family member or a friend, whom you have had a disagreement with, or where there is an unresolved issue? Decide to sort that out this week.*
- *Do you know someone who is lonely, or feeling left out, maybe at school or in a group which you belong to? What can you do to make them feel part of the community?*

Encourage the young people to commit to doing something during the next week in which they will act as a Christian in a way that they find difficult. Ideally this should be as a result of their own notes about real life and faith. The action can be very small and hidden if they want. They can write the action down in their journal but they do not need to share it with the group at all.

Tell the young people that at each session they will be asked if they have done their action and whether they want to share their experience with the group. Remind them that they do not have to share or tell anyone about their action if they do not want to.

Group action:
Is there anything we can do as a group to take action on what you have been discussing today?

What can we pray about?

You can encourage the young people to see praying as one way of taking action as a group.

Ask everyone to: write a very simple intention (e.g. "for victims of bullying","for my little sister who is ill", etc.) on a small piece of paper. These will be used during the closing prayer.

> **TIP** If the young people are planning a service project, there may be things they've noticed in today's discussion which they could help do something about.

Before you begin the closing prayer section, encourage the young people to read through and fill in their journal during the week ahead. Remind them that it is a tool to help them on their journey to confirmation. Their journal contains lots more information and ideas than can be covered in each section.

> **TIP** Remind the group that, at the next session, you will tell the group what name you have chosen as a confirmation name and will tell everyone a bit about the saint who shares that name. You will also be asked to name your sponsor and explain why you have chosen them.

QUOTE "Faith is to believe what you do not see; the reward of this faith is to see what you believe." *Saint Augustine*

PRAYER

You will need the candle and a basket or bowl for the prayer intentions.

This short prayer and meditation can be done in church with candles lit and lights dimmed. Perhaps you could all gather in church, sitting on the floor close to the altar. If using the church isn't practical you could instead sit in a circle around the candle as at the beginning of the session. You can use all the prayer and meditation below or just the prayer if you prefer. You might find it helpful to have meditative music in the background and perhaps an image – whether a photo, a statue, an icon or a Bible – beside the candle and basket to act as a prayer focus.

Ask the young people to put their prayer intentions in the basket. They don't need to tell anyone what they have written. Invite the group to become still. Light the prayer candle again.

> **TIP** " Why not ask different people to pray these prayers out loud? "

Our God, who is three in one, Father, Son and Holy Spirit,
Be present here with us as we pray.
Strengthen our belief and our faith.
Inspire us and bring us to the fullness of life which you offer to us all.
Amen.

Silence for a short while.

Read the following excerpt from the Gospel of St John (John 3:16)
For this is how God loved the world:
He gave his only Son,
So that everyone who believes in him may not perish
But may have eternal life.
For God sent his Son into the world
Not to judge the world,
But so that through him the world might be saved.

Final Prayer
Thank you God for the love you have shown me.
There are going to be times when I doubt you.
When this happens, please help me to come back to you
And to feel the love which you bring into our lives.
Amen.

As you end the session, remind the candidates of the date and time of the next session.

SESSION 8

Preparing the Confirmation Mass

Session 8
Preparing the Confirmation Mass

Aim:
To prepare the readings and prayers for the Confirmation Mass and to have a run through of the rite of confirmation.

Leader's reflection:
Do you remember your confirmation? What sticks in your mind? How did you feel on the day? What has being a confirmed Christian meant in the rest of your life?

In this session, you will help your group to plan the readings and prayers for their Confirmation Mass and do a run through of the rite of confirmation. By getting them involved in the preparation you are helping them to make this special occasion really their own. By doing the run through you will hopefully allay some of their apprehension about going into the unknown as their big day approaches.

> **TIP** " Maybe you could have a discussion with all the catechists about what each of you remembers about your confirmation. "

You will need:
- Flip-chart paper and pens
- A candle and something to light it with
- Some relaxing/meditative music
- Small pieces of paper for the young people to write their prayer intentions on and some pens/pencils to write with
- A basket or something to place the prayer intentions in at the end of the session

Candidates will need:
- Their candidate journal and a pen

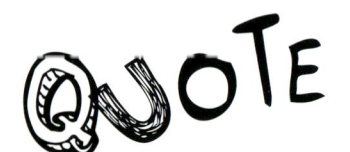

QUOTE "Send out your Spirit and life begins; you renew the face of the earth." *From Psalm 104*

Notes and ideas for catechists

This session contains suggestions for how to prepare for the Confirmation Mass with your group. However, different parishes have different ways of doing things. You may need to adapt what is in this session to fit the way your parish/deanery or diocese organise their confirmations. Obviously there's not a lot of point spending time choosing readings if your group can't actually use their own choices!

- If you are celebrating the sacrament of confirmation together with other parishes, you may need to talk to the catechists in those parishes to negotiate about who gets to choose what (e.g. perhaps one parish chooses the readings, another writes and reads the bidding prayers, another brings up the gifts at the offertory or hands out the Mass booklets at the beginning of Mass).
- You will need to check with your parish priest whether he is happy for your group to choose their own readings and/or bidding prayers before you go ahead with planning this with your group.
- This session includes thinking about choosing a confirmation name and choosing a sponsor. The group were asked to make their choices in Session 2. You might want to remind them of this a week or two ahead of this session in case they have not organised a sponsor or chosen a name.
- If your parish wants to produce a very professional looking Mass leaflet, you may need to hold this session earlier in the confirmation preparation process to allow time for the booklets to be printed.
- There are suggested readings in Appendix 2 to help you, but there are more suggested readings in the Lectionary if you should want to widen the choice.

QUOTE *"Christians must lean on the Cross of Christ just as travellers lean on a staff when they begin a long journey."* St Anthony of Padua

SEE

In this section we encourage the young people to examine the things that happen to them in their lives.

How are you feeling about your confirmation?

Ask the group to get into small groups and write down on flip charts what words and images come into their minds when they think about receiving the sacrament of confirmation. Encourage them to be honest. They may be anxious, excited, bored.

- **Now ask the group to discuss together: "Do you think it is important to commit yourself to being a Christian? Why?"**

Ask the group to get into small groups and write their thoughts down on flip charts to feed back to the group.

- **What have you chosen as your Confirmation name? Why did you choose this name? Do you know anything about the saint who had this name?**

Ask the young people to share this within their small groups, ask them to write their chosen name in their candidate's journals and ask them to list the names they have chosen on flip chart paper so you can display them on the wall during the rest of the session.

- **Who have you chosen as your sponsor? Why have you chosen him or her?**

Ask the young people to share this verbally within their small groups. They can write the answers down in their journals.

QUOTE

"You must be as lighted lanterns and shine like brilliant chandeliers among people. By your good example and your words, animate others to know and love God." *St Mary Joseph Rossello*

JUDGE

Do not do this section if your group will not be able to use their own choice of readings in their Confirmation Mass.

In Appendix 2 there is a selection of readings suggested for a Confirmation Mass. You may wish to photocopy the pages of readings to give to the group; alternatively you could give them Bibles to look up the passages in. We have given two choices for each reading and psalm, but there are more choices available in the Lectionary if you want to offer your group a wider selection.

A: Choosing the readings for the Confirmation Mass

Split your group into four smaller groups. Each small group is to concentrate on one of the readings. So group 1 will look at the choices of first reading, group 2 looks at the choices of second reading, group 3 looks at the psalm choices (this might be a sung or spoken psalm), group 4 looks at the Gospel.

Ask them to sit quietly reading the two suggested passages for their reading. Then taking one reading at a time ask them to answer the following questions:

- What happened in the reading?
- What does this say about being confirmed?
- Do you like this reading?

Once they have discussed both readings, ask them to choose the one they feel is best for their Confirmation Mass. Gather as a whole group and ask each group to read out and explain their preferred reading. Why do they think this reading is appropriate for their Mass?

Now as a whole group consider whether all the readings will work together. If not, consider which other choices could be made for the Mass. Ask for volunteers and choose readers for the Confirmation Mass for the first and second readings and, if you are having a spoken psalm, the psalm too (though this can be the person who reads the first reading).

> **TIP** " You need to make clear to your group that the Liturgy of the Word all needs to work together. This isn't a pick and mix of favourite bits of the Bible, it is a liturgy which is helping them to be ready to receive the sacrament of confirmation. "

B: Rehearsing the rite of confirmation

If the Confirmation Mass is going to take place in your parish church, take the young people into the church for this rehearsal. Even if the Mass is to take place in another church/cathedral you might still find it helps the young people to have this practice in your church.

Once you are in the church, explain to your group how they are going to be seated at the Mass and any other logistical information they need to know (e.g. do you want the candidates to gather in the church hall before the Mass begins? Where will the readers sit/stand, how long is the whole Mass likely to take?).

You could photocopy and share the text of the rite of confirmation in Appendix 2 so that each candidate can see a copy.

Rehearse any parts of the Mass you think your group needs to run through (you could include reading the readings and bidding prayers, or taking up the gifts at the offertory, as well as the rite of confirmation if you want to). The part which most candidates will be feeling nervous about is the rite of confirmation itself. When you run through the rite of confirmation, one of the catechists could volunteer to take on the bishop's role and stand in front of the altar, laying their hands on each candidate so that they know what this involves. Explain that although it is called "laying on", the bishop will extend his hands over them, not actually touching them. You could also demonstrate what is involved in being anointed with the oil of chrism.

QUOTE

"There is a variety of gifts but always the same Spirit; there are all sorts of service to be done, but always to the same Lord; working in all sorts of different ways in different people."

From St Paul's first letter to the Corinthians

ACE — Deciding on your action

Ask the young people whether they did the action they decided on at last week's session.

Ask the young people how they found doing their action.

> **Tell the group:**
> Today we have prepared for your Confirmation Mass. But now we want to think about what happens after you have been confirmed. What commitment will you make to your new life as a confirmed Christian?

Encourage the young people to think about what they intend to do to keep their faith alive after their confirmation. They can write their ideas in their journals.

> *To get their ideas started you could make some suggestions or ask some questions. Perhaps they could continue to meet as a group (there is a suggestion for this in Appendix 3 of this book), perhaps they have organised a service project which will continue after they are confirmed, perhaps there is a*

group in school they could join, or roles in the parish they could take on. Perhaps they could commit to attending Mass regularly (you might encourage them to attend a particular Mass with the opportunity for them to meet up afterwards for coffee).

At this point remind them that there is one more session of this group to attend after their confirmation. Remind them of the time and date of this meeting (you might like to combine that session with something social which the group could suggest).

QUOTE
"Those whose hearts are pure are temples of the Holy Spirit." St Lucy

Group action – preparing the bidding prayers

Decide how many bidding prayers you will need and split your group so that there is one group per prayer. People often feel nervous about writing prayers, so it may help to give them some guidance on topics for prayers (and make sure no two groups pick the same topic). Topics could include:

- World and Church leaders
- The confirmation candidates
- All those around the world being confirmed this year
- The school community
- The parish community
- Those who are suffering from… (this could be from illness, poverty, disability, discrimination, bullying, a recent news event such as a war or natural disaster, etc.)

Give them time to choose their topic (or you can give them topics if you prefer). Then ask them to draft their prayer onto flip-chart paper so everyone can see. If you have enough catechists, it might be useful to have one catechist per group to help guide them in how to write a prayer. Ask for a volunteer from each group to read their prayer in the Mass (try to make sure it isn't the same people who are doing the readings). Get the whole group to share their prayers once they are all written.

TIP
Writing your prayers

Lord,
We pray for … (subject)
That … (intention)
Lord hear us / Lord in your mercy

e.g. Lord,
We pray for everyone being confirmed this year
That their hearts may be filled with love for you and for one another.
Lord hear us.

QUOTE

"Trying to do the Lord's work in your own strength is the most confusing, exhausting, and tedious of all work. But when you are filled with the Holy Spirit, then the ministry of Jesus just flows out of you."
Corrie ten Boom

PRAYER

This short prayer and meditation can be done in church with candles lit and lights dimmed. Perhaps you could all gather on the sanctuary, sitting on the floor in front of the altar. If using the church isn't practical you could instead sit in a circle around the candle as at the beginning of the session. You can use all the prayer and meditation below or just the prayer if you prefer. You might find it helpful to have meditative music in the background and perhaps an image – whether a photo, a statue, an icon or a Bible – beside the candle and basket to act as a prayer focus.

> Lord Jesus,
> When you returned to heaven from earth, you promised to send your Holy Spirit to dwell within your followers. Make us worthy in our hearts, so that we will be ready to receive the gifts of the Spirit when we receive the sacrament of confirmation.
> Amen.

Silence for a short while

Read the following prayer which is attributed to St Patrick

> Christ with me, Christ before me, Christ behind me,
> Christ in me, Christ beneath me, Christ above me,
> Christ on my right, Christ on my left,
> Christ when I lie down, Christ when I sit down, Christ when I arise,
> Christ in the heart of every man who thinks of me,
> Christ in the mouth of everyone who speaks of me,
> Christ in every eye that sees me,
> Christ in every ear that hears me.

Final Prayer

> Loving Father,
> In the days before my confirmation, may I concentrate on the sacrament I will receive so that the celebration may be full of joy; and may I not be too distracted by all the new clothes and parties which surround it. Thank you for the time we have had in this group preparing for our confirmation. May we always draw strength and comfort from what we have learned together.
> Amen.

As you end the session, remind the candidates of the date and time of their Confirmation Mass, and any other logistical information they will need to know before the day.

SESSION 9

Actively Living Life

Session 9
Actively Living Life

Aim:
To follow up on their confirmation by thinking about how the young people can live their faith as Christian leaders.

Leader's reflection:
Now you have spent some time with this group of young people, what have you noticed about them? Think about the characters you have encountered. How do you feel about the way each of them has approached their confirmation? On their confirmation day, did you feel proud of them? Today it is time to say goodbye and send the group out on their big adventure: the rest of their lives. Inspire them to make Jesus central to each of them.

> **TIP:** Try to meet with all the catechists to have a de-brief session. Review how the course went this year and think about what you might do differently next year. Try to get your learning in writing so that if there are any new catechists next year, they will have something to refer to.

You will need:
- A candle and something to light it with
- Some relaxing/meditative music
- Flip-chart paper and pens
- Small pieces of paper for the young people to write their prayer intentions on and some pens/pencils to write with
- A basket or something to place the prayer intentions in at the end of the session

Candidates will need:
- Their candidate journal and a pen

QUOTE: "You will go out with joy and be led away in safety. Mountains and hills will break into joyful cries before you and all the trees of the countryside clap their hands." *From the book of Isaiah*

Begin with a prayer…

As the young people begin to arrive have the lights in the room dimmed, a candle lit in the centre. As each person arrives, invite them to sit quietly in a circle around the candle. Perhaps play some reflective music in the background.

> Lord Jesus,
> Thank you for the gifts of your Holy Spirit which we received at our confirmation. Thank you for the love of our family and friends and all those who came to support us on our confirmation day. Now that we have been confirmed, strengthen us as we move forward into our new lives as confirmed Christians.
> Amen.

TIP " This prayer is also printed in the candidates' books. Perhaps ask a volunteer to pray it out loud while everyone adopts a posture of their choice, conducive to prayer. "

To get us started…

To get everyone started, begin with a group exercise to help everyone feel comfortable in each other's company. Use the following activity, or another one of your choice.

Ask one person to volunteer as the "leader".

TIP " If you have a big group, split into smaller groups of roughly 10 people for this task. "

Ask the rest of the group to join hands and form a circle. Then, without letting go of each other's hands, invite them to move over, under, and between each other to form a human knot. Encourage them to get into as much of a tangle as possible, but not to let go of one another's hands.

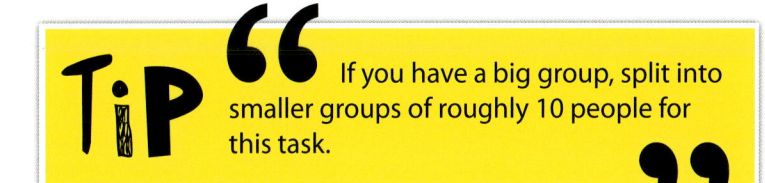

Now invite the "leader" to untie them, back into a circle once again without anyone letting go of one another's hands. Everyone must follow the leader's instructions cooperatively. No one should move unless told to do so. Keep track of the time it takes.

Repeat it a second time. The leader can join if he or she wishes. This time invite the group to untie the knot by themselves. (It should be simpler and quicker.)

Compare the time it takes with and without the leader trying to direct things.

Once the group is settled again, ask them what they thought the activity was about. They will probably comment on teamwork, cooperation, not relying on one person, etc. Allow this to lead to a discussion on the issue of leadership and working together. We often think of a leader being someone who tells others what to do, when in fact we are all leaders in our lives and the lives of others and together can make the biggest difference. The game also shows that even when we have got ourselves into a mess, by sticking together, all part of the same chain, we can get ourselves out of the situation again.

SEE

In this section we encourage the young people to examine the things that happen to them in their lives.

What has happened to you this week that has made you think or caused you concern?

Ask each young person to think about one thing that has happened to them this week and to write in down it their journal. Ask them to share this in pairs and then with the whole group.

Invite a member of the group to chart up the responses on a flip chart.

Now ask everyone to get into small groups and discuss the following questions
- What do you think a leader is?
- How do you spot a leader? What qualities does he/she have?
- Do you know any good leaders?
- What do they do?
- What is special about them?

Ask one person in each group to write down the group's thoughts on flip-chart paper. Then share with the whole group.

Say to the group:
There are so many areas and situations in life where we can see that help is needed. We need people who will make a difference… people who will lead lives that will transform the world. Confirmed Catholics, like yourselves, are called to lead those lives.

We are surrounded all the time by people leading us, or trying to! Whether at school, home, or in your part-time jobs, there is always somebody ready to "lead" us in how to live our lives. The media presents us with people in government who tell us how to act. But there are lots of other more subtle ways in which we are led: by fashion, by advertising, by peers and by other people's expectations of us.

In small groups ask the young people to discuss the following:

Who and what do you think people your age are prepared to be led by?

Again get answers on flip-chart paper and feed back responses to the whole group.

JUDGE

A: Gospel enquiry

Invite the group to listen carefully to the story and to think about the time, place and people involved. Perhaps you could ask a member of the group to read. The Gospel text is printed in their journals.

Read the Gospel, Mark 10:41-45
"When the other ten heard this they began to feel indignant with James and John, so Jesus called them to him and said to them, 'You know that among the gentiles those they call their rulers lord it over them, and their great men make their authority felt. Among you this is not to happen. No; anyone who wants to become great among you must be your servant, and anyone who wants to be first among you must be slave to all. For the Son of man himself came not to be served but to serve, and to give his life as a ransom for many.'"

And discuss together…
- Who is in this story?
- What happened?
- What was said?
- How do you think the apostles present would have reacted to this? Why?
- What kind of life is Jesus calling us to lead in this Gospel story?

Leader's ideas:
This reading comes from just before Jesus and his disciples arrive in Jerusalem. By now Jesus has become famous and is drawing large crowds to hear him speak. His apostles, James and John, had asked Jesus to give them special places in heaven, but Jesus has told them that although they can share his life, they will not be granted special favours.

Throughout the Gospels Jesus always turns things on their head! If we want to be great, we must be a servant, if we want to be first, we must be last!

Jesus is not saying that we cannot do great things, but rather that we must not use our achievements as a way of overshadowing others. Everything that we do should be for the benefit of those around us, and never at anyone else's expense. At your confirmation you said to the whole Church and to God that you want to share in the life of Jesus. And Jesus has shown us, by the way he lived, that the way to share in his life is to love our neighbours.

B: What does our faith say?

As baptised and confirmed Catholic Christians, we are called to **lead** our lives in a certain way; that is to say that we are called to always follow Jesus Christ as The Way. We are also called to be leaders in our own lives. But the type of **leaders** we are meant to be is very different from the type of leaders we often see around us in the world.

Get into small groups and discuss the following questions:
- What do you think a Christian leader is?
- What qualities do they have?

Feed back responses to the whole group.

C: Why bother?

Sometimes we look around us at the world and think that our lives cannot make a difference. The world just has too many problems. After all, what we do won't be noticed anyway. But there are loads of examples of people who really have made a difference. And each one of us can make the world a better place to live in even if it is just in small ways.

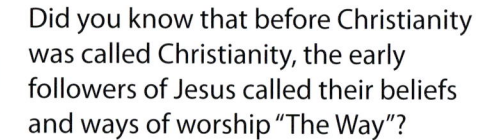

GLOSSARY

Did you know that before Christianity was called Christianity, the early followers of Jesus called their beliefs and ways of worship "The Way"?

Mother Teresa only ever did small things. She reached out to the poor she saw around her, by leaving her religious order and using her basic medical training to tend to those in need. Gradually she built up a religious community of fellow nuns to work with the poor in Calcutta (now Kolkata), the Indian city where she lived. As she saw needs, she tried to meet them through medical care, education, orphanages and food distribution. She did not set out to establish a global organization but that is what she did, little by little. Her order, the Missionaries of Charity, now have missions in 120 countries around the world.

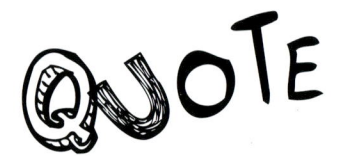

QUOTE "We ourselves feel that what we are doing is just a drop in the ocean. But if that drop was not in the ocean, I think the ocean would be less because of that missing drop. I do not agree with the big way of doing things." *Mother Teresa of Calcutta (1910-1997)*

Ask the group to read the information above (it is printed in their journals) and then to discuss the following questions:

- What do you think about the quotation Mother Teresa gave?
- Mother Teresa was serving the poor in Calcutta because that's where she saw the need.

    What situations did you share at the beginning of the session?
    Do you see the need to make a difference?

Ask someone in the group to write down the answers to the next question on a flip chart.

- What situations might you be called to be leaders in?

Discuss the answers as a whole group.

ACT

Deciding on your action

So far we have looked at how we have been given a role as confirmed Catholics and we have explored what that leadership role might mean for each of us. When we look at how our real lives and faith combine, it leads to action. Once we have thought through God's perspective on our lives we are ready to decide on an action.

Personal action:

Encourage the young people to think back to before their confirmation day when they last decided on an action as a result of a confirmation preparation session. Did they manage to do it? If so, how did it go?

Tell the group:
Now you have been confirmed, it is time to go out and begin your new lives as confirmed Christians. Each one of you is called in different ways to follow Jesus and to use the gifts of the Holy Spirit as Christian leaders.

Think back to the situations we discussed earlier. Have a look at the first flip-chart page about your concerns this week. Is there anything you can do in these areas to try and live as Christian leaders?

Encourage the young people to commit to doing something during the next week and in the weeks, months and years ahead in which they will act as Christian leaders. Ideally this should be as a result of their own notes about real life and faith. The action can be very small and hidden if they want. They can write the action down in their journal but they do not need to share it with the group at all unless they want to.

Group action:

Is there anything we can do as a group to take action on what you have been discussing today? Have a look also at the flip chart about what things your age group are prepared to be led by. What group actions can you take which will be examples of being led by something worthwhile?

Where do you want to go next as a group?

In Appendix 3 there are details of organisations who help groups of young people to continue to meet after confirmation. Impact (part of the YCW movement) uses the same SEE, JUDGE, ACT method as this programme. The other organisations also help young people to continue to meet, to grow in faith, and to put their faith into practice.

Encourage the group to commit to meet again to decide how to continue. Don't delay. It's always best to invite whoever is interested to meet in the next week or two, whilst the group is still enthusiastic. You might want to invite a young person to volunteer to find out information about the organisations in time for the meeting.

What can we pray about?

You can encourage the young people to see praying as one way of taking action as a group.

Ask everyone to: write a very simple intention (e.g. "for victims of bullying", "for my little sister who is ill", etc.) on a small piece of paper. These will be used during the closing prayer.

> **TIP** " If the young people are planning a social get-together as a group they could use this as an "action" and plan it as part of this session. "

Before you begin the closing prayer section, encourage the young people to hang onto their journals and to refer to them whenever they need reminding about what they have learned.

Thank the young people for their time, commitment and energy and give them a chance to thank all the catechists (including yourself).

QUOTE

"Love God, serve God: everything is in that."
St Clare of Assisi

PRAYER

You will need the candle and a basket or bowl for the prayer intentions.

As this is the final gathering of this group, you might want to expand this prayer session or ask the young people to come up with their own prayers which they say aloud to the group.

This prayer and meditation can be done in church with candles lit and lights dimmed. Perhaps you could all gather in church, sitting on the floor close to the altar. If using the church isn't practical you could instead sit in a circle around the candle as at the beginning of the session. You can use all the prayer and meditation below, or just the prayer if you prefer. You might find it helpful to have meditative music in the background and perhaps an image – whether a photo, a statue, an icon or a Bible – beside the candle and basket to act as a prayer focus.

Ask the young people to put their prayer intentions in the basket. They don't need to tell anyone what they have written. Invite the group to become still. Light the prayer candle again.

> **TIP** " Why not ask different people to pray these prayers out loud? "

We gather here to pray together for the last time in this group.
After each line of this prayer, we all respond by saying: "Thank you, Lord."

For all the fun we have had. **Thank you, Lord.**
For all that we have learned. **Thank you, Lord.**
For the times when we have prayed together. **Thank you, Lord.**
And for the memories we have gathered. **Thank you, Lord.**
Amen.

Silence for a short while

Read the following excerpt from Psalm 100

Cry out with joy to the Lord, all the earth.
Serve the Lord with gladness.
Come before him, singing for joy.

Know that he, the Lord, is God.
He made us, we belong to him,
We are his people, the sheep of his flock.

Go within his gates, giving thanks.
Enter his courts with songs of praise.
Give thanks to him and bless his name.

Indeed, how good is the Lord,
Eternal his merciful love.
He is faithful from age to age.

Final Prayer

Thank you, Lord,
for this group and all that we have done together.
Now it is time for us to leave
and to find our own ways to follow you for the rest of our lives.
Guide us and strengthen us through gifts of your Holy Spirit.
May we always know your love
and find comfort in our faith and trust in you.
Amen.

Appendix 1: A Service of Reconciliation

This is to be used in conjunction with Session 5 (Preparing for Reconciliation).

The content in orange is optional. You need to use the sections which are written in black, although you can choose alternative readings or prayers.

A Hymn

All make the **sign of the cross**

The priest greets everyone present.
(Use this greeting or another of your choosing or your priest's)

Grace and peace be with you
from God the Father
and from Jesus Christ
who loved us
and washed away our sins in his blood.
R: And also with you

Opening prayer
(use this one or another of your choosing)

Lord,
Hear the prayers of those who call on you,
Forgive the sins of those who confess to you,
And in your merciful love
give us your pardon and your peace.
We ask this through Christ our Lord.
R: Amen

Introduction
(this could be done by a priest or a catechist)

Let's think about the last few sessions we have had together. We have looked at the difficulties we have in life. We have asked ourselves what principles we should hold as Christians. We have thought about how our lives could and should be different from non-Christians. Today is our chance to reflect on how well we have done at living how Jesus wants us to live. It is a chance to look at our lives and to admit where we have failed to live up to the principles and actions which we know are right.

Let us take a few moments to reflect on what we have learned in the last few weeks.
What do you now know is important to you? What does God ask of you?
What do you know to be right? What have you done wrong?

Liturgy of the Word

Choose at least one scripture reading. If you are only having one reading, choose a Gospel reading. A selection is given below but you can choose others as appropriate.

New Testament Readings

A reading from the letter to the Romans. **Romans 12:9-12**

Do not let your love be a pretence, but sincerely prefer good to evil. Love each other as much as brothers should, and have a profound respect for each other. Work for the Lord with untiring effort and with great earnestness of spirit. If you have hope, this will make you cheerful. Do not give up if trials come; and keep on praying.

A reading from the second letter of St Peter. **2 Peter 1: 3-7**

By his divine power, Jesus Christ has given us all the things that we need for life and for true devotion, bringing us to know God himself, who has called us by his own glory and goodness. In making these gifts, he has given us the guarantee of something very great and wonderful to come: through them you will be able to share the divine nature and to escape corruption in a world that is sunk in vice. But to attain this, you will have to do your utmost yourselves, adding goodness to the faith that you have, understanding to your goodness, self-control to your understanding, patience to your self-control, true devotion to your patience, kindness… and to this kindness, love.

Psalms *(you could replace the psalm with a hymn or a period of silence if you wish.)*

Psalm 51

*Have mercy on me, God, in your kindness.
In your compassion blot out my offence.
O wash me more and more from my guilt
And cleanse me from my sin.*

*My offences truly I know them;
My sin is always before me.
Against you, you alone, have I sinned;
What is evil in your sight I have done.*

*Indeed you love truth in the heart;
Then in the secret of my heart teach me wisdom.
O purify me, then I shall be clean;
O wash me, I shall be whiter than snow.*

*A pure heart create for me, O God,
Put a steadfast spirit within me.
Do not cast me away from your presence,
Nor deprive me of your holy spirit.*

Psalm 138

*O Lord, you search me and you know me,
you know my resting and my rising,
you discern my purpose from afar.
You mark when I walk or lie down,
all my ways lie open to you.*

*For it was you who created my being,
knit me together in my mother's womb.
I thank you for the wonder of my being,
for the wonders of all your creation.*

*Already you knew my soul,
my body held no secret from you
when I was being fashioned in secret
and moulded in the depths of the earth.*

*O search me, God, and know my heart.
O test me and know my thoughts.
See that I follow not the wrong path
and lead me in the path of life eternal.*

Gospel Readings

A reading from the holy Gospel according to Matthew
Matthew 9:9-13
As Jesus was walking on he saw a man named Matthew sitting by the customs house, and he said to him, "Follow me". And he got up and followed him.
While he was at dinner in the house it happened that a number of tax collectors and sinners came to sit at the table with Jesus and his disciples. When the Pharisees saw this, they said to his disciples, "Why does your master eat with tax collectors and sinners?" When he heard this he replied, "It is not the healthy who need the doctor, but the sick. Go and learn the meaning of the words: what I want is mercy, not sacrifice. And indeed I did not come to call the virtuous, but sinners."

A reading from the holy Gospel according to Luke
Luke 7:36-50
One of the Pharisees invited Jesus to a meal. When he arrived at the Pharisee's house and took his place at table, a woman came in, who had a bad name in the town. She had heard he was dining with the Pharisee and had brought with her an alabaster jar of ointment. She waited behind him at his feet, weeping, and her tears fell on his feet, and she wiped them away with her hair; then she covered his feet with kisses and anointed them with the ointment.

When the Pharisee who had invited him saw this he said to himself, "If this man were a prophet, he would know who this woman is that is touching him, and what a bad name she has."… Jesus said, "I tell you that her sins, her many sins, must have been forgiven her, or she would not have shown such great love." Then he said to her, "Your sins are forgiven… Your faith has saved you; go in peace."

A reading from the holy Gospel according to John
John 15:9-12
Jesus said to his disciples:
"As the Father has loved me,
so I have loved you.
Remain in my love,
Just as I have kept my Father's commandments
And remain in his love.
I have told you this
So that my own joy may be in you
And your joy be complete.
This is my commandment:
Love one another,
As I have loved you."

If you are going to have a homily, it will be given here.

Examination of Conscience
This could be a formal one of your priest's choosing, or the activity in the IDEAS boxes (p.112), or something similar. There are many guides for teenage Examination of Conscience available on the Internet, which you could suggest to your priest.

General Confession
You can use the traditional prayer below or another if you prefer (with your priest's approval)

I confess to almighty God,
and to you,
my brothers and sisters,
that I have greatly sinned,
in my thoughts and in my words,
in what I have done
and in what I have failed to do,
through my fault, through my fault,
through my most grevious fault;
therefore I ask blessed Mary,
ever virgin,
all the angels and saints,
and you,
my brothers and sisters,
to pray for me to the Lord our God.

The Our Father

Individual confessions
You could sing hymns here or have music playing in the background whilst each person goes to make their confession.

Thanksgiving
This could be one of the activities in the IDEAS boxes, a hymn, a period of silence, or a formal prayer chosen by your priest.

Final Prayer
Your priest will choose a prayer to finish.

You can sing a final hymn if you wish.

IDEAS

Light a Candle

You will need: a candle for each candidate, something to put the candles in once they are lit (this could be a candle stand in front of a statue which is already in your church).

After each candidate has received absolution and returned to their seat and performed their act of penance they can get up one at a time and light a candle at a central point.

IDEAS

Washing your sins away

This activity can be done as the examination of conscience and the thanksgiving parts of the service if your priest is happy to do this.

You will need: pieces of thin paper, pencils, a large vase (preferably glass) or bowl, food colouring, water, glass jug of bleach.

Give squares of paper and a small pencil to each candidate. Play some quiet music in the background and ask the candidates directly, "How have you done wrong? How have you failed in your love for others and in your love for God?" They can write down any number of responses, as they wish, but will probably write at least two or three.

They should keep these pieces of paper to use in the act of thanksgiving after they have made their individual confessions.

Ask everyone to fold their pieces of paper on which they have written their sins and place them into the vase or bowl of coloured water. Once they are all in the vase/bowl you can reflect on how the sacrament of reconciliation restores us again to a loving relationship with each other and with God, just as it was on the day of our baptism. Add in bleach and watch the water turn clear and see their "sins" washed clean. The bleach in the glass jug represents the water of our baptism, through which we were welcomed into the loving and forgiving family of God. (You will want to do a trial run of this before the service, just to check that the bleach will work with the kind of ink or food colouring you have coloured the water with: blue dye in particular often doesn't go clear!)

IDEAS

Cross of Ribbons

You will need: a plain wooden cross, enough red and white ribbons for one of each for each candidate.

After each candidate has received absolution and returned to their seat and performed their act of penance they can get up one at a time and pin a small red ribbon to a plain wooden cross. Once they have pinned their red ribbon on the cross (signifying how Christ took on the burden of our sins on the cross) each candidate can take away a white ribbon from a bowl below the cross (signifying their renewed relationship with God and each other).

Appendix 2: The Confirmation Mass, some suggested texts

This is to be used in conjunction with Session 8 (Preparing the Confirmation Mass).

Liturgy of the Word
You must choose a first and second reading, a psalm (though this could be a hymn) and a Gospel reading. Two choices for each are given below.

First Readings
If the Confirmation Mass is taking place outside the Easter season, choose one of the two Old Testament readings. If the Confirmation Mass is taking place in the Easter season, choose one of the two New Testament readings within this "First Readings" section to be the first reading.

EITHER A

A reading from the prophet Isaiah
Isaiah 61:1-3.6.8-9

The spirit of the Lord has been given to me,
for the Lord has anointed me.
He has sent me to bring good news to the poor,
to bind up hearts that are broken;
to proclaim liberty to the captives,
freedom to those in prison;
to proclaim a year of favour from the Lord,
a day of vengeance for our God,
to comfort all those who mourn and to give them
for ashes a garland;
for mourning robe the oil of gladness,
for despondency, praise.
But you, you will be named "priests of the Lord",
they will call you "ministers of our God".
I reward them faithfully and make an everlasting covenant with them.
Their race will be famous throughout the nations,
their descendants throughout the peoples.
All who see them will admit that they are a race whom the Lord has blessed.

This is the word of the Lord.
R: Thanks be to God

OR B
A reading from the prophet Joel
Joel 2:23.26 – 3.3

Sons of Zion, be glad, rejoice in the Lord your God. You will eat to your heart's content, will eat your fill, and praise the name of your God who has treated you so wonderfully. My people will not be disappointed any more.

And you will know that I am in the midst of Israel, that I am the Lord your God, with none equal to me. My people will not be disappointed any more.

After this I will pour out my spirit on all mankind. Your sons and daughters shall prophesy, your old men shall dream dreams, and your young men see visions.

This is the word of the Lord.

OR IN EASTER SEASON

EITHER A
A reading from the Acts of the Apostles
Acts 1:3-8

Jesus had shown himself alive to the apostles after his Passion by many demonstrations: for forty days he had continued to appear to them and tell them about the kingdom of God. When he had been at table with them, he had told them not to leave Jerusalem, but to wait there for what the Father had promised. "It is" he had said "what you have heard me speak about: John baptized with water but you, not many days from now, will be baptised with the Holy Spirit."

Now having met together, they asked him, "Lord, has the time come? Are you going to restore the kingdom to Israel?" He replied, "It is not for you to know times or dates that the Father has decided by his own authority, but you will receive power when the Holy Spirit comes on you, and then you will be my witnesses not only in Jerusalem but throughout Judaea and Samaria and indeed to the ends of the earth."

This is the word of the Lord.

OR B
A reading from the Acts of the Apostles
Acts 2:1-6. 14. 22-23. 32-33

When Pentecost day came round, the apostles had all met in one room, when suddenly they heard what sounded like a powerful wind from heaven, the noise of which filled the entire house in which they were sitting; and something appeared to them that seemed like tongues of fire; these separated and came to rest on the head of each of them. They were all filled with the Holy Spirit, and began to speak foreign languages as the Spirit gave them the gift of speech.

Now there were devout men living in Jerusalem from every nation under heaven, and at this sound they all assembled, each one bewildered to hear these men speaking his own language.

Then Peter stood up with the Eleven and addressed them in a loud voice:
"Men of Judaea, and all you who live in Jerusalem, make no mistake about this, but listen carefully to what I say. Jesus the Nazarene was a man commended to you by God by the miracles and portents and signs that God worked through him when he was among you, as you all know. This man, who was put into your power by the deliberate intention and foreknowledge of God, you took and had crucified by men outside the Law. God raised this man Jesus to life, and all of us are witnesses to that. Now raised to the heights by God's right hand, he has received from the Father the Holy Spirit, who was promised, and what you see and hear is the outpouring of that Spirit."

This is the word of the Lord.

Psalms [you could replace the Psalm with an appropriate hymn if you wished.]

EITHER

Psalm 103
R/ Send forth your Spirit, O Lord,
And renew the face of the earth.

Bless the Lord, my soul!
Lord God, how great you are.
How many are your works, O Lord!
In wisdom you have made them all.
The earth is full of your riches. R/

All of these look to you
To give them their food in due season.
You give it, they gather it up:
You open your hand, they have their fill. R/

You send forth your spirit, they are created;
And you renew the face of the earth.
May the glory of the Lord last for ever!
May the Lord rejoice in his works! R/

I will sing to the Lord all my life,
Make music to my God while I live.
May my thoughts be pleasing to him.
I find my joy in the Lord. R/

OR

Psalm 22
R/ The Lord is my shepherd;
there is nothing I shall want.

The Lord is my shepherd;
There is nothing I shall want.
Fresh and green are the pastures
Where he gives me repose.
Near restful waters he leads me,
To revive my drooping spirit. R/

He guides me along the right path;
He is true to his name.
If I should walk in the valley of darkness
No evil would I fear.
You are there with your crook and your staff;
With these you give me comfort. R/

You have prepared a banquet for me
In the sight of my foes.
My head you have anointed with oil;
My cup is overflowing. R/

Surely goodness and kindness shall follow me
All the days of my life.
In the Lord's own house shall I dwell
For ever and ever. R/

Second Readings

EITHER A
A reading from the letter of St Paul to the Romans
Romans 8:26-27

The Spirit comes to help us in our weakness. For when we cannot choose words in order to pray properly, the Spirit himself expresses our plea in a way that could never be put into words, and God who knows everything in our hearts knows perfectly well what he means, and that the pleas of the saints expressed by the Spirit are according to the mind of God.

This is the word of the Lord.

OR B
A reading from the letter of St Paul to the Ephesians
Ephesians 4:1-6

I, the prisoner of the Lord, implore you to lead a life worthy of your vocation. Bear with one another charitably, in complete selflessness, gentleness and patience. Do all you can to preserve the unity of the Spirit by the peace that binds you all together. There is one Body, one Spirit, just as you were all called into one and the same hope when you were called. There is one Lord, one faith, one baptism, and one God who is Father of all, over all, through all and within all.

This is the word of the Lord.

Gospel Readings

EITHER A
Gospel Acclamation

Alleluia, alleluia!
Come, Holy Spirit, fill the hearts of your faithful,
And kindle in them the fire of your love.
Alleluia!

A reading from the holy Gospel according to Matthew
Matthew 5:1-12

Seeing the crowds, Jesus went up the hill. There he sat down and was joined by his disciples. Then he began to speak. This is what he taught them:
"How happy are the poor in spirit;
theirs is the kingdom of heaven.
Happy the gentle:
they shall have the earth for their heritage.
Happy those who mourn:
they shall be comforted.
Happy those who hunger and thirst for what is right:
they shall be satisfied.
Happy the merciful:
they shall have mercy shown them.
Happy the pure in heart:
they shall see God.
Happy the peacemakers:
they shall be called sons of God.
Happy those who are persecuted in the cause of right:
theirs is the kingdom of heaven.

"Happy are you when people abuse you and persecute you and speak all kinds of calumny against you on my account. Rejoice and be glad, for your reward will be great in heaven."

This is the Gospel of the Lord.

OR B
Gospel Acclamation

Alleluia, alleluia!
The Father will give you another Advocate
To be with you for ever, says the Lord.
Alleluia!

A reading from the holy Gospel according to John
John 14:15-17

Jesus said to his disciples:
"If you love me you will keep my commandments.
I shall ask the Father,
and he will give you another Advocate
to be with you for ever,
that Spirit of truth
whom the world can never receive
since it neither sees nor knows him;
but you know him,
because he is with you, he is in you."

This is the Gospel of the Lord.

The Rite of Confirmation

All stand, and the bishop (B) questions the confirmands (C), who all reply together.

B: Do you reject Satan and all his works and all his empty promises?

C: I do.

B: Do you believe in God the Father almighty, creator of heaven and earth?

C: I do.

B: Do you believe in Jesus Christ, his only Son, our Lord,
who was born of the virgin Mary, was crucified, died and was buried,
rose from the dead,
and is now seated at the right hand of the Father?

C: I do.

B: Do you believe in the Holy Spirit,
the Lord, the giver of life,
who came upon the apostles at Pentecost
and today is given to you sacramentally in confirmation?

C: I do.

B: Do you believe in the holy catholic Church,
the communion of saints, the forgiveness of sins,
the resurrection of the body, and life everlasting?

C: I do.

B: This is our faith. This is the faith of the Church.
We are proud to profess it in Christ Jesus our Lord.

All: Amen.

The Laying on of Hands
Concelebrating priests stand near the bishop. He faces the people and with hands joined, says:

B: My dear friends:
in baptism God our Father gave the new birth of eternal life
to his chosen sons and daughters.
Let us pray to our Father
that he will pour out the Holy Spirit
to strengthen his sons and daughters with his gifts
and anoint them to be more like Christ the Son of God.

All pray in silence for a short time.

The bishop and the priests who will minister the sacrament with him lay hands upon all the candidates (by extending their hands over them). The bishop alone says:

B: All-powerful God, Father of our Lord Jesus Christ,
by water and the Holy Spirit
you freed your sons and daughters from sin
and gave them new life.
Send your Holy Spirit upon them
to be their helper and Guide;
give them the spirit of wisdom and understanding,
the spirit of right judgement and courage,
the spirit of knowledge and reverence.
Fill them with the spirit of wonder and awe in your presence.
We ask this through Christ our Lord.

All: Amen.

The Anointing with Chrism
The sponsor places his/her right hand on the candidate's shoulder and gives the candidate's confirmation name to the bishop (or the candidate may give his/her own confirmation name).

The bishop dips his right thumb in the chrism and makes the sign of the cross on the forehead of the one to be confirmed, as he says:

B: N., be sealed with the Gift of the Holy Spirit.
C: Amen.

B: Peace be with you.
C: And also with you.

The Blessing

At the end of Mass, in place of the usual blessing, the following blessing may be used.

B: God our Father
Made you his children by water and the Holy Spirit:
May he bless you
And watch over you with his fatherly love.

All: Amen.

B: Jesus Christ the Son of God
Promised that the Spirit of truth
Would be with his Church for ever:
May he bless you and give you courage
In professing the true faith.

All: Amen.

B: The Holy Spirit
Came down upon the disciples
And set their hearts on fire with love:
May he bless you,
Keep you one in faith and love
And bring you to the joy of God's kingdom.

All: Amen.

B: May almighty God bless you,
The Father, and the Son, and the Holy Spirit.

All: Amen.

Appendix 3:
Resources to support a group after confirmation

This confirmation programme, *Truth*, has used the process of See-Judge-Act to enable young people to make the link between their life and their faith. It was developed by Cardinal Joseph Cardijn as part of his "Pastoral Response" to address the needs that young people faced almost one hundred years ago. Cardijn saw that to link life and faith, there was a need for an organised approach, which trained young people to transform their own lives and the lives of others around them. This organised approach he called the Young Christian Workers (YCW). The Young Christian Workers remains the largest youth movement in the Catholic Church today, in nearly sixty countries across the world.

The YCW exists to help form young people to be actively involved in their lives; to become a leader in life. Leader is not used in the sense of the head of a group, but rather in the sense of the Christian leader, as the apostle of Christ, who is engaged and proactive in their own surroundings. This is a model of leadership, a leadership in life, and is ideal for an approach to teenage confirmation. It helps to enable young people to recognise their own worth and to live a life of true meaning and value. It helps us to address the reality that no matter how many times candidates are told about the faith, unless they accept it into their everyday life situations, it will have little lasting effect.

The resources listed below are recommended for your group to use if they wish to follow up their confirmation programme. These resources can help to introduce Cardinal Cardijn's full method to your young people.

After being a member of YCW myself, becoming its National President, and now as a catechist and adult companion to members of YCW, I have one very strong piece of advice: start now and don't worry about numbers. There is always the temptation to wait until after the holidays, or after exams, or after whatever. The truth is that it is much harder to start again (even in two or three months) than it is to continue to meet next week. If you are reading this, you are probably looking to continue with your group of young people after confirmation, and I would encourage you do to that – continue, and resist the temptation to stop for a break. If only a small number of young people turn up, don't worry. It is perfect. From a small beginning great things will come. I have seen plenty of groups start from one young person. If one turns up, he or she most likely needs the Church's visible support, and you continuing to meet will show that. And it is most probably he or she who will bring others over the coming months to join you.

Danny Curtin

The YCW offers three main resources to help you get started.

Take Out Pizza Box: The perfect way to get started, Take Out includes everything you need in a pizza box to 'take out' an action and transform your local community. Over 4 to 6 weeks, reflect on life and faith (including a DVD Scripture reflection), and plan an action to make a difference.

The Impact Pack
Everything needed to start a YCW Impact group for teenagers (aged 13-17). A multimedia 'Start-up Kit', with DVD containing clips for weekly meetings, will engage and inspire young people, plus the pack contains a comprehensive adult companion's guide. The pack provides up to two years' worth of weekly resources.

Challenge to lead
A complete pack for a YCW group (aged 16-25), including a year's worth of material for weekly meetings. The DVD and themed enquiries, on issues relevant to young adults' lives today, will help young people link their life and faith through action.

More information and other resources are available from

YCW
St Joseph's
off St Joseph's Grove
Hendon
NW4 4TY

020 8203 6290
info@ycwimapct.com
www.ycwimpact.com

Other resources and support

There are other organisations who will be happy to help your group to develop. They will be able to provide you with resources to help facilitate your group's enthusiasm for various topics.

CAFOD
CAFOD is the Catholic Agency for Overseas Development. They provide resources and support for young people and youth leaders.

cafod.org.uk/greatgeneration
Introduce global justice to young people and help inspire them to be part of a great generation, responding through fundraising, campaigning and prayer to support those in need.

cafod.org.uk/youthleaders
A complete toolkit for young leaders. Perfect for inspiring promising young leaders from your confirmation group to help engage themselves and their peers in promoting global justice.

Pax Christi Youth
The work of Pax Christi - the Peace of Christ - is based on the Gospel and inspired by faith. Their vision is of a world where people can live in peace, without fear of violence in any form. Pax Christi Youth organise peacemaking events for young people and provide resources for groups. For more information see www.paxchristi.org.uk

Catholic Youth Ministry Federation (CYMFed)
www.cymfed.org
CYMFed is the national body which brings together all the diocesan and national organisations which work with young people in the Church. Through CYMFed you can contact your local diocesan youth office for help, support and ideas, or contact other organisations, such as the Youth SVP, which will provide other follow-up methods for working with your group after confirmation.